CAPTAIN TOM MOORE

A LIFE STORY

Sally Morgan

Illustrated by Sarah Papworth

SCHOLASTIC

To my mum, Diane Pilkington, and to everyone who
lost a loved one during Covid – "We'll Meet Again"

First published by Scholastic in the UK, 2021
Euston House, 24 Eversholt Street, London, NW1 1DB
Scholastic Ireland, 89E Lagan Road, Dublin Industrial Estate, Glasnevin,
Dublin, D11 HP5F

SCHOLASTIC and associated logos are trademarks and/or
registered trademarks of Scholastic Inc.

Text © Sally Morgan, 2021
Illustrations by Sarah Papworth

ISBN 978 0702 31232 8

Printed in the UK by CPI Group UK (Ltd), Croydon, CR0 4YY
Paper made from wood grown in sustainable forests and other controlled
sources.

1 3 5 7 9 10 8 6 4 2

www.scholastic.co.uk

CONTENTS

AN ENEMY LIKE NO OTHER

On 23 March 2020, Prime Minister Boris Johnson announced to the nation that the United Kingdom was facing a threat unlike anything seen on British shores for over a century. The country was under attack from an unseen enemy. An enemy with the potential to leave many thousands of people dead. The enemy was a virus known as the COVID-19 virus. COVID-19, was first identified in Wuhan, China in 2019, but spread quickly. It was now spreading within the United Kingdom.

Boris announcing lockdown

For months, the UK government watched as COVID-19 spread around the world, infecting hundreds of thousands of people and devastating the healthcare systems of the countries it passed through. The new virus was highly infectious and affected people in different ways. Some people got very sick very quickly, with symptoms which included coughing, severe shortness of breath and a high fever. However, as scientists learned more about the virus, they discovered some people reported subtler symptoms such as a loss of taste and smell, and stomach problems such as vomiting and diarrhoea. Even more mysteriously, some people infected by the virus had no symptoms at all but were still capable of passing it on to others.

Finding out more

Scientists all over the globe dropped what they were doing and set to work studying the virus to find out more about how it spread and why it affected people in such different ways. They needed to devise tests that could be performed quickly to find out who had the virus and who didn't. They needed to find out how the virus passed from person to person. They needed to design systems for telling people if they had been in contact with an infected person and whether they needed stay away from others. They needed to find medicines that were effective at treating people with the virus, and most importantly of all, they needed to formulate a vaccine to prevent people from catching the disease in the first place.

While scientists worked around the clock to unravel the mysterious virus, doctors and nurses in National Health Service (NHS) hospitals worked tirelessly to treat the people who came through their doors. The most severely ill patients filled the beds in intensive care units quickly. These patients were put on machines called ventilators, which helped them breathe while their bodies fought off the virus. The doctors and nurses did everything they could, but as more people contracted the virus it became harder and harder for them to keep up with the number of people needing help. Soon it would be impossible – there would be no more beds or ventilators for those who needed them. Something needed to be done – and fast.

THE FIGHT AGAINST COVID-19

National Lockdown

To give scientists more time to find solutions and to take the pressure off the NHS, Prime Minister Boris Johnson told the nation he needed everybody's help to slow the spread of the disease and save lives.

"FROM THIS EVENING I MUST GIVE THE BRITISH PEOPLE A VERY SIMPLE INSTRUCTION – YOU MUST STAY AT HOME."

Boris Johnson

People were only allowed to leave their homes to go to work (if they were unable to work from home), shop for essential items, exercise, or provide care for a vulnerable person.

The decision had not been easy. For weeks the government watched as countries around Europe locked down to prevent the spread of the virus. The UK government had hoped they would be able to avoid it, by recommending people wash their hands and stay two metres (six feet) apart, but it hadn't been enough. The virus was spreading quickly, the hospitals were full, people were dying and the NHS was at risk of collapse.

The government hoped that keeping people in their homes as much as possible would slow the virus passing from person to person and take the pressure off the NHS. They also hoped it would give them a chance to buy more equipment, such as ventilators and protective clothing for hospital staff, search for new treatments, work on a vaccine and roll out a testing system.

"EACH AND EVERY ONE OF US IS NOW OBLIGED TO JOIN TOGETHER. TO HALT THE SPREAD OF THIS DISEASE. TO PROTECT OUR NHS AND TO SAVE MANY, MANY THOUSANDS OF LIVES. AND I KNOW THAT AS THEY HAVE IN THE PAST SO MANY TIMES, THE PEOPLE OF THIS COUNTRY WILL RISE TO THAT CHALLENGE. AND WE WILL COME THROUGH IT STRONGER THAN EVER. WE WILL BEAT THE CORONAVIRUS AND WE WILL BEAT IT TOGETHER. AND THEREFORE

I URGE YOU AT THIS MOMENT OF NATIONAL EMERGENCY TO STAY AT HOME, PROTECT OUR NHS AND SAVE LIVES."

Boris Johnson

Life at home

While it became known as a "national lockdown", nobody was really locked inside their homes, even if they felt like they were. They were allowed to get out to exercise, go to work and shop for essentials, but they were not allowed to gather with others. This national lockdown meant different things for different people.

People in Lockdown

For children, lockdown meant that unless their parents were essential workers they couldn't go to school. Instead, they had to learn at home, either using electronic devices, such as smartphones or computers, or completing paper assignments sent home by their teachers.

Lockdown meant not being to play with their friends or go round to their houses. It meant no birthday party get-togethers. For many, lockdown meant not being able to see their grandparents or any family members who didn't live with them.

For parents, lockdown meant working from home if they were able, while trying to look after and teach their children. It meant worrying about older relatives that didn't live in the household. For many people, with so many businesses closed, it also meant worrying about whether they would lose their jobs.

For people who lived alone, it meant not seeing anyone at all. No cups of tea with friends and no hugs.

For elderly people, and people with health conditions that made them more at risk from the virus, lockdown meant no visits from friends, family or grandchildren.

Lockdown made many people lonely, frightened and stressed. The prime minister assured people that that government was working as hard as it could to make sure the measures would last as short a time as possible, but with cases of the virus on the rise no one knew when it would end.

Rising to the Challenge

It was a difficult time for everyone, but the nation rose to the challenge, just as the prime minister had asked them to. People came up with clever ways to distract themselves and others from their worries. People got together using video call apps such as Zoom, Houseparty and Google Meet.

Video call party

Children had playdates with friends, LEGO challenges, watch parties, discos and even karaoke parties together online. Adults set up family meals on video calls and even hosted dinner parties with their friends, all using a phone, tablet or laptop and a few pots and pans. People all over the country set themselves challenges to get through the days. Some attempted to learn a new hobby, such as painting or playing a musical instrument, while others learned new languages. Some set themselves fitness challenges.

A Personal Challenge

For one ninety-nine-year-old man in the Bedfordshire village of Marston Moretaine, lockdown was far from lonely. Captain Tom Moore lived with his daughter Hannah, her husband, Colin, and their two children Benjie and Georgia. For Captain Tom life was similar to how it had been before lockdown, except that everyone in the family now had to stay home. His routine stayed the same. He woke up early, dressed and rode his stairlift down to the kitchen to make porridge. After breakfast, Captain Tom did his exercises. He'd always liked to be active, but now exercise was more important than it had ever been. Captain Tom was recovering from a broken hip and ribs caused by a near fatal accident in 2018. After his accident, Captain Tom was treated by kind doctors and nurses in an NHS hospital and rehabilitation centre. Both they and Captain Tom had worked hard to help him get better, and while he was well enough to now be back at home, Captain Tom's injuries made walking difficult and often painful. Before his accident, Captain Tom led a busy and independent life, and he knew that if he wanted to get back to that he needed to move as much as he could. So, he walked.

Captain Tom walking

On 6 April 2020, Captain Tom Moore decided to do his exercises in the spring air. He stepped outside with his frame and began to walk the length of his garden. From the other side of the garden, his son-in-law Colin joked he would give Tom one pound per lap, something Tom had done to encourage his grandchildren's sporting achievements. Colin said Tom should try to do one hundred laps before his hundredth birthday, to raise money for charity. Captain Tom thought this was a wonderful idea; he had raised money before and it was just the motivation he needed to keep going.

A Hero Like No Other

Captain Tom knew where he would donate the money to: all the doctors and nurses of the NHS. Doctors and nurses like the ones who had treated him after his accident, who had cared for his wife in her final years, and been there for his family and so many others, whenever the need arose. Doctors and nurses like the ones who were working on the front lines to treat people in the worst pandemic the world had seen for a hundred years.

Captain Tom knew what it was like to fight on the front lines. He had fought a different kind of enemy on the front line in Burma during World War Two. Captain Tom wasn't able to fight any more, but he could walk ... just. Could he walk a hundred laps of his garden? Tom wasn't sure if he could, but he was sure he wanted to do something to help people who were putting their lives on the line to help so many others.

His daughter Hannah thought Captain Tom's walk would be the kind of story that could bring a bit of joy into people's lives, so she sent a press release to the local television station in the hope that they would pick up the story and perhaps help to raise a little more money than the family could by themselves. What happened next was beyond their wildest dreams. After appearing on a local news programme, other channels picked up the story. Soon instead of local news, Captain Tom's walk was national news, and from one small interview, Captain Tom and Hannah were giving more than ten interviews a day to television and radio networks all over the world. Some days, Captain Tom even appeared on breakfast television before eating his own porridge, but he loved it.

Breakfast T.V. interview

Captain Tom felt encouraged by the attention he was getting and it motivated him to continue. He loved that he was doing something useful and raising money for a charity close to his heart and he loved that he was bringing joy to people's lives.

A Beacon of Light

With all the media attention, it was hard for Captain Tom to fit the reason for it – his walk – into his schedule, but he managed it, a bit at a time. It wasn't easy. Captain Tom completed the final steps of his walk on 16 April 2020 and by his birthday on 30 April he had raised more than £30 million for NHS Charities Together.

Captain Tom completes his walk

When Captain Tom started his walk, he wasn't sure if he would be able to do it, but he knew he wanted to try. He was slow and sometimes his steps were very painful, but he was determined.

It was this determination that led Captain Tom to have a year unlike any other and bring a little bit of light and hope into the lives of people all over the United Kingdom and the world.

With all the media attention focused on Captain Tom on his one hundredth birthday, people wanted to know more about the man who had captured the world's imagination. Who was he and what had he been doing for the ninety-nine years and eleven months before he became a national treasure? And what, after such an achievement, did he intend to do next?

FIRST STEPS

Thomas Moore was born at home on 30 April 1920 in Keighley, Yorkshire, to Isabella and Wilfred Moore. Keighley was a mill town which specialized in the spinning and weaving of wool and cotton, as well as machinery. Tom's father, Wilfred Moore, worked for the family building firm and Tom's mother, Bella, had worked as a head teacher at a local school before getting married. Wilfred and Bella named Tom after his grandfather, Thomas Moore.

THOMAS MOORE AND SONS

Wilfred's father, Thomas Moore, was a local celebrity. Despite being unable to read or write, he had worked hard to become a master builder and set up a successful building firm called Thomas Moore and Sons.

To begin with, Thomas took on odd jobs like building walls, but eventually moved up to building houses and even monuments. One of these monuments included one of the country's first memorials to the soldiers lost during World War One. The memorial was unveiled in 1924 and stands in Keighley to this day.

Thomas built a house for his family, which he named Club Nook. He was an ambitious and determined man whose company provided jobs for people in the community, including his two sons, Wilfred and Billy. Wilfred was proud of his father, which is why he decided to name his son after him.

Wilfred had entered the family business when he left school at fourteen joining his older brother, Billy, who already worked there. Wilfred didn't want to work for the family business for ever. He was a keen photographer and hoped to turn his favourite hobby into a career. His plans changed, however, after he contracted a virus when he was twenty-one years old. Wilfred was so poorly his family wasn't sure he would survive. In the end, Wilfred was lucky. He recovered from the illness, but the virus left him almost completely deaf.

Wilfred never found out which virus he'd had or what had caused him to lose his hearing, but his life would never be the same. In today's world, Wilfred would have the opportunity to learn sign language and be able to access all manner of tests and electronic hearing devices. He would also be able to connect with the deaf community and be offered tools and support to help him adjust. But at the start of the twentieth century, the healthcare system and people's attitudes towards disability were different to what we know today. In the early 1900s, people with disabilities were treated badly and often excluded from society. Wilfred's dreams of becoming a photographer were no longer within his reach.

Wilfred and his family had to work out what to do themselves. Wilfred taught himself to read people's lips to work out what they were saying. When this wasn't possible, he relied on a member of the family to shout into his good ear.

HEALTHCARE AROUND 1900

Today if you feel ill or have a nasty fall at the park and need stitches or a plaster cast, your parent or guardian can take you to your GP or call an ambulance to take you to hospital for urgent treatment.

If you were unwell at the turn of the century, things were very different. Most patients had to pay for healthcare, so how well looked after you were depended on how much money you had. If you had a lot of money, you could call for a doctor to come and see you at your house, but this was very expensive. If you didn't have money, you would have to rely on unreliable medicines made at home. If you were very ill, you might be taken to a poorhouse or workhouse, where there may have been a nurse on duty.

A poorhouse, or workhouse, was a place where people who had little money, or were unable to work due to old age or disability, could find food and shelter in return for long hours of hard work. Conditions in the poorhouse were bad and the people who operated them were often cruel. In 1929, new laws meant local authorities could turn poorhouses into hospitals funded by charitable organizations.

Not only was seeing a doctor in the 1920s expensive, but if you needed medicine, that would cost even more. Today, if you go to the doctor and they think you have an infection such as tonsillitis or conjunctivitis, you will often be given a prescription for medicines known as antibiotics. Antibiotics are excellent at clearing up bacterial infections very quickly, but they weren't discovered until 1929. Before antibiotics and other modern medicines, common infections could make patients unwell for a very long time. They could even be fatal.

Life at Clark Road

Tom lived with his parents and his older sister, Freda, in a two-bedroom house on Clark Road in Keighley. Unlike houses today, Tom's house did not have electricity. Instead, at night the family used candles or lamps that were powered by gas. Tom's house, unlike many houses at the time, did have the luxury of an indoor toilet and bathroom.

ELECTRICITY IN 1920

In 1919, only about six per cent of homes in the UK had electric lighting, but things were changing. Electric light was not only much safer than gas and oil lamps, it was also cleaner and brighter. By 1939, almost two thirds of homes had electricity.

Tom and Freda liked living in Clark Road because it wasn't far from their grandparents. Bella's mother, who Tom and Freda called Granny Fanny, lived just down the road with Tom's uncle Arthur. Wilfred's father lived in Club Nook, a few kilometres away in a village called Riddlesden, next door to Tom's uncle Billy.

Tom and Freda got on well, and they made friends with other children who lived on their street. They loved to play but didn't have many toys. Wilfred didn't believe in buying his children toys, which he thought were a waste of money. Instead, he brought home tools and materials from his work. Rather than toy cars or teddy bears, Tom was given a hammer, nails, a saw and pieces of wood. With these (and a little bit of help) Tom could make all the toy trucks he wanted.

tools.

"HE'D SHOW ME HOW TO BANG THE NAILS INTO THE WOOD. AND IF YOU HIT YOUR THUMB, THAT WAS YOUR OWN FAULT AND YOU LEARNED NOT TO DO IT AGAIN. AND WHEN I WAS FINISHED WITH THOSE, MY FATHER WOULD BRING ME A BIGGER PIECE OF WOOD AND A BIGGER HAMMER."

Captain Sir Tom Moore

When Tom was five years old, he started at the local school, which Freda already attended. Their school was about a mile away and Tom and Freda cycled there and back each day. Tom enjoyed school and was very well behaved, partly because he was scared of being sent to see the head teacher, but also because he liked his class teacher, Miss Moffit. Tom liked his lessons and taking part in school plays, but he hated school dinners! Instead of eating at school, Tom and Freda would cycle home, where their mother would have a delicious lunch of meat and potatoes waiting for them. Tom thought his mum was a brilliant cook, baker and an even better teacher.

Little Chef

Tom loved his mum's food so much that she thought he should learn how to make it himself. Tom's dad, like many men at the time, did not know how to cook, and relied on his wife to prepare his meals. Bella was determined that Tom would be able to look after himself if he needed to. She taught her son not only how to make cakes and biscuits but how to make proper meals, like the roast dinners they had on Sundays.

Tom's mum wasn't the only cook in the family. Granny Fanny and Uncle Arthur were both excellent cooks too. Uncle Arthur was a pastry chef who could make all kinds of fancy cakes and desserts. He also told Tom funny stories that would make him laugh. Granny Fanny made delicious oat biscuits and let him eat lumps of sugar from the sugar bowl. Granny Fanny had a box of handwritten recipes for everything, from biscuits to home remedies for ailments including the common cold and back pain.

Tom and Freda didn't need these remedies often as they were rarely ill. This was lucky because whenever they were ill, they either had to swallow down one of Granny Fanny's less-than-lovely remedies or, if that didn't work, their father would buy a foul-tasting bottle of medicine called "fever cure" from the pharmacy. Wilfred expected his children to be better by the time the bottle was finished.

This method worked well until Tom was too ill for Granny Fanny's remedies or his father's fever cure. Thankfully Tom's parents had the money to take him to a doctor. Tom was diagnosed with scarlet fever and needed to go to hospital. Even though he was only little, his parents were not allowed to stay with him in the hospital. Tom was infectious so he had to be quarantined on an isolation ward where his parents could only wave to him through a window.

Young Tom

SCARLET FEVER

Scarlet fever is a bacterial infection that is easily treated today with antibiotics.

Symptoms of scarlet fever include a high temperature (called a fever), a sore throat and a red rash that covers most of the body. In the 1920s, scarlet fever was often fatal and killed many hundreds of children in the UK each year. Scarlet fever is caught by breathing in bacteria in droplets exhaled by an infected person. It can also be transmitted by sharing towels or touching the skin of someone infected with the bacteria that causes the disease.

Eventually, Tom was well enough to leave hospital and made a full recovery at home. It wasn't too long before he was able to go back to school and play outside with his friends again. Tom loved being outdoors. He liked to explore the dales around Keighley where he would collect tadpoles and other slimy specimens to bring home to his mum – who wasn't always happy to see them.

On the Road

Unlike most families at this time, Tom and his family got the chance to explore even further. In the mid 1920s, the business was doing well, and Wilfred had earned enough money to buy a motorcar so they could travel on road trips around the country. Wilfred was determined his children should learn how to read maps and navigate. Tom knew how to find his way around the countryside where they lived by using features in the landscape to help him, but navigating while hurtling down the road in a motorcar was a different matter. Before they set off, Wilfred would hand either Tom or Freda

Rover 8 car

the map and let them choose where they were going to go that day. Tom and Freda travelled all over Yorkshire, across the Dales and to the coast, trying to navigate while being peppered with questions about things they saw along the way by their father. Bella learned how to drive, too. Tom thought his mother was a better driver than his father, but wasn't sure if that was because she was better able to hear his and Freda's directions. Freda and Tom became excellent map readers, a skill that they would both rely on when they got older.

CARS IN 1920

In the early twentieth century, motorcars were still a fairly new invention. Owning a car was a real luxury. In 1920, there were fewer than one million cars on Britain's roads compared to 40.1 million registered vehicles today. Instead, the roads were filled with bicycles and horses and carts, just like the ones used by Thomas Moore and Sons to transport building materials. Goods were moved around the country by rail or barge.

As well as taking day trips, Tom's family went on holiday together in the car. In a town like Keighley, workers and their families were given one week's holiday a year. People would save money all year in order to be able to afford to travel to seaside towns such as Whitby and Blackpool.

Tom looked forward to his annual holiday. He loved playing at the beach with his sister and fishing off the end of the pier. When they caught a fish, they took it back to their boarding house where the landlady would cook it for their breakfast. As well as paddling and fishing, there were puppet shows, a fairground and donkey rides to enjoy. One holiday, Tom got to ride something more exciting than a helter-skelter or a donkey when his mother bought him a ticket to ride in a small aeroplane. It was Tom's first time in an aeroplane, and it didn't look much like one you would see today. It was a biplane used during

World War One, but now instead of fighting, it was used to take paying holidaymakers on pleasure rides up and down the bay. After Bella bought his ticket, Tom climbed into the passenger seat. Tom was nervous, even though he had seen the pilot take off and land countless times.

Biplane

Once they were in the air Tom was amazed at how small everything looked down below. All too soon, it was time for the pilot to land. But Tom's excitement wasn't over yet; as the plane landed in the field it tipped over on to a wing and had to be set back on its wheels before he was able to climb out. The bumpy landing didn't spoil Tom's trip one bit; he wished he could have flown higher and for longer.

A Boy's Best Friend

When Tom was eight, Uncle Billy gave him a very special present. Tom's uncle believed that every boy should have a dog and so he bought Tom a friendly cocker spaniel. Tom was delighted and named his new friend Billy, after his uncle.

Tom and his dog Billy soon became best friends. They went everywhere together, taking long walks across the Yorkshire Dales. Tom would pack a lunch and leave with Billy right after breakfast, walking for miles and not coming home until teatime.

As much as Tom loved his dog, he loved his uncle even more. Uncle Billy worked with his dad and his grandad at the family building firm during the week. At weekends, he liked to ride motorcycles. Billy was a daring and skilled rider who took part in off-road races all over Yorkshire. The routes across the Dales, up muddy hills and through streams, were designed to put the rider and the motorcycle to the ultimate test, and accidents were common. People flocked to see the daring riders compete. Billy was a champion and his stunts, such as riding across a canal on a narrow wooden plank, were often featured in the local newspaper.

Billy on his bike

When Billy wasn't racing motorcycles, he enjoyed taking them apart. Uncle Billy's house had a cellar which he used as a workshop. Billy's workshop was filled with motorcycle parts and tools. It was a mess, but Tom thought it was brilliant.

Motorcycles were very popular in the 1920s. There were more than three hundred motorcycle manufacturers in the United Kingdom. They didn't cost as much as motorcars, so they weren't out of reach for working class people looking for something a bit more exciting than a bicycle, but far less expensive than a car. They were also easy to repair which meant people could ride them hard and fix them relatively quickly themselves.

As well as motorbikes, Uncle Billy also loved cars, which he kept in his garage and worked on often. Tom was fascinated by how things worked. He spent time with Uncle Billy, tinkering with engines and learning everything he could from him about how they worked. Tom dreamed that one day he would have a motorcycle of his own and race it around the countryside, just like his uncle did. Until that day came, he was happy spending time with Billy and learning what he could.

Aside from his dog, Tom's best friend was a boy called Walter who lived on his street. They played football together, rode their bikes and had games of kick can – a simple game for two or more people, where one player kicks a can in the street and everyone races to get to where it lands. The aim is to reach it first and to be the one to kick the can again.

Father and Son Time

When Tom wasn't at school, playing or helping Uncle Billy, he enjoyed going to the cinema with his father. Going to the cinema in the 1920s was very different to going to the cinema today. All the films were in black and white and didn't have sound until nearly the end of the decade, so you couldn't hear what the actors were saying. Instead, the actors' lines flashed up on the screen, and music played over the top. Tom's favourite films were cowboy films.

The cinema was something Tom and his father could enjoy together. Because the actors' lines were written on the screen, Tom and Wilfred could watch the film without Wilfred having to ask Tom what was being said. Tom also enjoyed the dramatic piano music that accompanied the film.

The Moores had a piano at their house on

Clark Road. Tom's dad had learned to play the piano before he lost his hearing and liked to play for the family. Bella, Freda and Tom would stand around the piano and sing together.

Tom and his father got on well, but Tom found it hard to talk to him about his problems or things that were worrying him, because he always had to shout. Tom knew he could go to his mother when he needed advice, but when he felt he needed another man to talk to, he would cycle over to Uncle Billy's.

A NEW HOME

In August 1931, the Moores got some very sad news. Grandfather Thomas had died. Thomas was loved by his family and respected by everyone who knew him. He was remembered not only for the buildings and monuments constructed by Thomas Moore and Sons, but also for being a good and fair employer who provided well-paid jobs for people who worked in the town, including many men who had been injured during World War One. Grandfather Thomas had started the company from nothing. After he died, it became Billy and Wilfred's responsibility to take charge.

The death of Grandfather Thomas brought another big change for Tom and Freda – moving house. Grandfather Thomas left Club Nook to Wilfred and his family. Club Nook was much larger than Tom's house on Clark Road. It had a telephone, electricity and a large garden to play in. Even better than all that – it was right next door to Uncle Billy's house. Tom could now tinker with motorcycles and engines and chat with Uncle Billy to his heart's content.

Uncle Billy and Tom went to motorcycle races together and discussed the articles in Uncle Billy's many motorcycle magazines. However, as much as Tom enjoyed working with Uncle Billy on his motorcycles, it wasn't the same as having one of his own. He hadn't given up on his dream of being a motorcycle owner just yet.

A Lucky Find

In 1932, when Tom was about twelve, he was out on a walk with his friend Walter and dog Billy, when they came across an old barn. Tom and Walter went inside and in a dusty corner, Tom found an old, broken-down motorcycle. It was rusty and needed new tires. "Its tyres were flat, it was covered in dust and didn't run," he later remembered. The motorcycle was a mess, but that didn't matter to Tom. He asked the owner of the barn if he could buy it and paid half a crown, which is about fourteen pounds in today's money!

Brough superior SS-80 motorbike.

Tom pushed the bike home and spent the next few months stripping it down, cleaning the parts and putting it back together again. Nobody offered to help him, but Tom didn't need it. Instead, he put all the skills he'd learned from his father's practical presents and the hours he had spent helping Uncle Billy in his workshop to good use. Eventually, thanks to Tom's mechanical knowhow and a lot of trial and error, the bike ran. But as Tom was only twelve, he was too young to get his motorcycle licence and take it out on the road. Instead, he rode his bike out in the fields around Club Nook. Tom put the old bike through its paces whenever he got the chance. It broke down every now and again, but Tom just took it apart and fixed it.

By this time, Tom was going to the local grammar school. Students were split into groups depending on how good they were at different subjects and whether or not the teachers thought they would do well at university. Tom was good at practical subjects, such as woodwork and engineering, so he was put in a group with other students who wanted to learn a trade. If Tom did well, he would earn an apprenticeship at a local business when he left school. An apprentice is someone who learns how to do a job while working within the industry. Tom wasn't sure he would get picked for an apprenticeship though. He was brilliant at the practical subjects, but he still had to study academic subjects too. He didn't enjoy maths and only paid attention in French because he thought his teacher was very pretty.

Fortunately, Tom did earn an apprenticeship. He left school at fifteen to work as an apprentice at a local water engineering company. This job was ideal for Tom partly because he got to drive the company van. Directing his mother and father on their family outings was fun, but now it was his turn behind the wheel. Tom felt free as he drove around the countryside looking at plans for new water pipes, testing the water in rivers and streams and assessing the flow and pressure of water in people's homes.

Tom explored the outdoors in his spare time too, just as he had when he was a little boy. He joined the Youth Hostel Association (YHA).

YOUTH HOSTELLING

Tom, like many young people in the 1930s, loved to travel and be outdoors. The Youth Hostel Association was set up to provide safe, affordable accommodation to young people wanting to travel around Great Britain and explore the great outdoors. The first youth hostel opened its doors to travellers in 1930. By 1939, there were nearly 300 similar hostels dotted around the country, providing accommodation to over 83,000 members.

Tom also joined a local potholing club. Potholers explore systems of caves, often venturing far beneath the ground. Potholers use ladders, ropes and headlamps to help them find their way. Potholing can be dangerous. Today potholers wear helmets to help protect them from rockfalls. Tom and his friends only wore trilby hats – narrow-brimmed hats made from felt.

Life for Tom was changing and expanding. From playing in the streets around Clark Road and having childish adventures with his friends on the Yorkshire Dales, he now had a job, earned his own money and could travel all over the country. He was independent in other ways too: he could cook, read a map and drive, and he had been able to fix motorbikes by himself since he was twelve years old. Tom wasn't a boy any more. He was becoming a man.

Three years after the loss of his grandfather, Tom's world was shaken again when his uncle Billy died while working in his garage. This made Tom very sad. Tom had learned so much from his uncle. He was able to talk with him in a way he wasn't able to with his father.

Changes in Europe

The world was changing in other ways too. In 1933, a man named Adolf Hitler was elected chancellor of Germany. After their defeat in World War One, the German government signed a treaty which said they had to take responsibility and pay for the losses suffered by other countries during the war. This treaty was called the Treaty of Versailles. The Treaty of Versailles devastated the German economy already suffering from losses during the war. Unemployment in Germany skyrocketed, and many people couldn't afford food or a place to live.

Hitler and the Nazis rose to power by promising people an end to these hard times.

They promised to abolish the Treaty of Versailles and to make Germany, then a republic of different states, into a strong united nation under a single powerful ruler. They believed many of Germany's problems were caused by people they did not believe to be real Germans such as Jewish people living in the country. Hitler and the Nazis believed German people were superior to other people and believed that the German population could grow into a great empire, but to do this they needed more space. Hitler's plan, which he had described in books written the 1920s, was to invade much of Europe and by doing so take control of European territory overseas.

Hitler's plans were no secret. He made powerful speeches to his followers outlining his ideas for the German people. Many outside of Germany didn't like what they heard. They feared Germany was preparing for a war similar to World War One, which had rocked the world from 1914 to 1918 and cost nearly 20 million lives. To prevent this, the British, French and Polish governments agreed that they would come to one another's aid should Germany attack. These countries became known as the Allies. They hoped their strong alliance would deter Germany from making a move. Germany formed a similar agreement with Italy which became known as the Axis Alliance.

A Change in the Air

On 22 May 1936, a clear signal that Tom's life and the lives of many were about to change for ever appeared in the sky above Keighley. This signal was a 245-metre-long German airship called the *Hindenburg* which flew low over the town.

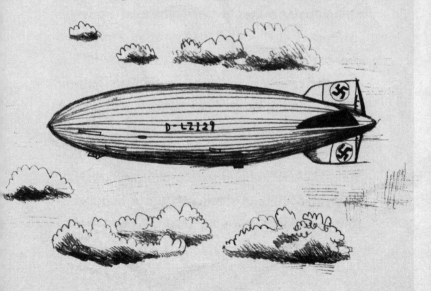

The *Hindenburg* was a hydrogen-filled German passenger airship, seen by the Nazis as a symbol of German strength and superiority. The Zeppelin Company launched their record-breaking flying machine in March 1936. The *Hindenburg* flew passengers across the Atlantic to the United States and Brazil. It was able to complete the journey in just two days, compared to more than a week aboard an ocean liner.

As well as being a transatlantic passenger airship, the *Hindenburg* was also used by the Nazi government for propaganda. Not only was a swastika, the symbol of the Nazi party, emblazoned on its lower fin, it was also fitted with enormous speakers, which broadcast messages in support of the Nazi leader, Adolf Hitler, and dropped propaganda leaflets to people on the ground. It made appearances at the 1936 Olympic Games and important Nazi rallies.

The *Hindenburg* flew over Keighley on its way back to Frankfurt, Germany from New York, USA. It stopped to deliver a package. The package contained a crucifix and a bouquet of flowers from a priest on board, named Father

Schulte. Also in the package was a note from Father Schulte, asking for the flowers to be placed on the grave of his brother, Lieutenant Franz Schulte. Lieutenant Schulte was a German airman captured during World War One and held as a prisoner in Skipton, Yorkshire. Lieutenant Schulte died on 2 March 1919 from the Spanish Influenza – following the 1918 Flu Pandemic. The package was picked up by Boy Scouts, Jack Gerrard aged eleven and Alfred Butler aged twelve who were on their way to a meeting when they saw the package drop. The boys took the package home to their parents before placing the flowers on the grave.

1918 FLU PANDEMIC

In February 1918, shortly before the end of World War One a dangerous strain of the influenza (flu) virus spread throughout the world. Symptoms of this dangerous new strain of flu included fever, aches and pains, nausea, difficulty breathing, dark spots on the face and a blue hue to the skin. Unlike most strains of the flu virus, which most severely affects the very old or very young, the 1918 influenza was most fatal in young healthy individuals. The flu spread quickly among the troops in their crowded camps and around the world as the tired soldiers returned home after the war ended in November 1918.

Between the years 1918–1920 more than 500 million people contracted the virus. Hospitals filled quickly and were soon overwhelmed. When the virus infected doctors and nurses and other frontline healthcare workers such as porters and paramedics, hospitals had to rely on medical students and volunteers. Between 50 and 100 million people across the world died, with 228,000 people dying in the United Kingdom alone.

Many saw the *Hindenburg*'s visit and the priest's package as an innocent act of remembrance from one brother to another, but others suspected a more sinister reason behind the fly-by. A writer in the Yorkshire Observer wrote that it was, "a wonderful opportunity for German pilots to look at our country and take note." But why would German pilots want to take a look at the country? Because many believed Germany was preparing for war. Signs for this included Germany increasing the size of its army from the 100,000 men permitted by the Treaty of Versailles, to 1.4 million and by manufacturing weapons to supply its expanding navy and air force.

As the threat of war loomed, towns around the country did what they could to prepare. If war was declared, there was a good chance that German bombers would fly over to England. In Keighley, men dug trench shelters in the park and the council advertised for volunteer air-raid wardens to look out for German bombers in the skies overhead. Government officials assessed local businesses to see if they could switch from their current industries to manufacturing things that would help the war effort, such as ammunition or military vehicles. Even the local Scouts were recruited to fill sandbags to help protect buildings, should they come under attack.

In March 1938, German troops marched into Austria and took control of the government. Many in Europe feared that this was just the beginning and that Germany had plans to invade other countries. It would turn out that they were right.

Despite the growing threat of war, Tom and his uncle Arthur took a trip to Switzerland. It was Tom's first holiday outside of England. He was excited to see the world and also to spend time with his uncle, who he was very close with. Arthur told funny stories and was a talented performer who sang with the local Gilbert and Sullivan society. Tom and Arthur travelled across Europe by train. As Arthur was a pastry chef and Tom a keen cook, the pair enjoyed trying new foods along the way.

When they got home, Arthur confessed to Tom's father that he had been worried that war might break out at any minute. In spite of this, the trip had made Tom hungry to explore more of the world. It wouldn't be long until Tom, and many other men his age, would get that chance – whether they wanted it or not.

Breaking News

At 11 o'clock on 3 September 1939, Tom sat with his parents around the wireless to listen to a very important announcement. Prime Minister

Neville Chamberlain, speaking from the cabinet room at 10 Downing Street, confirmed what many had feared – Britain was at war with Germany. On the day war was declared, the UK government passed a law that all men between the ages of eighteen and forty-one must register themselves as available for military service at their local recruitment office. This law was called conscription. Conscription had also been introduced during World War One. It was needed to make sure the British military had enough soldiers, sailors and pilots to fight a war.

Tom didn't hesitate and was among the first to sign up. He and many other young men felt it was their duty to defend their country and stand up for freedom. After registering, Tom needed to be assessed by a doctor to check he was fit and healthy. Then he waited to be assigned to a unit in the army, called a regiment. Some of his friends were called up right away, but Tom had to wait his turn.

While he waited, Tom joined the Riddlesden Local Defence Volunteers (LDV). The LDV's main job was to stay alert for any threat. The

LDV met every evening to patrol and keep watch for any unusual activity around the town or aircraft in the skies above. Many members of the LDV were veterans who had fought in World War One but were now too old to sign up to fight. These veterans taught new recruits such as Tom how to use a rifle and what to look out for when they were on patrol.

Tom wasn't the only member of his family to volunteer. Tom's uncle Arthur volunteered to drive lorries and ambulances. His sister, Freda, joined the Auxiliary Territorial Service (ATS). The ATS was the women's branch of the British Army. In 1939 women were not permitted to fight, but were given roles as cooks, radar and searchlight operators, and drivers of military vehicles. Later in the war, Freda got to use some of the map skills she learned in her father's motorcar when she worked as a plotter for the Women's Auxiliary Airforce (WAAF). A plotter marked the positions of fighter planes in a map room.

Life in Keighley changed fast. New rules, called rationing, controlled how much fuel and food people were allowed to buy. Blackout regulations, which had been put in place before war was declared, were stepped up. Blackout regulations included turning off streetlights, painting over car headlamps and hanging thick, black drapes over windows to stop light seeping into the street. These regulations protected the town from bombing by hiding it from German aircraft flying over at night. To confuse German spies who might be in the area, people took down road signs or painted over them. Some people dug trenches in their back gardens or built shelters to protect them from bombing raids.

The war also brought many new young residents to Keighley, and to other small towns and villages in the countryside, all over the United Kingdom. These were children evacuated from the big cities to protect them from bombing. The evacuees were invited to stay in people's homes. Tom's mum and dad hosted two evacuees at Club Nook. As well as hosting children, Keighley also converted its old workhouse into a home to host elderly people evacuated from London.

PRIVATE TOM
REPORTS FOR DUTY

In May 1940, Tom received a letter telling him that he had a few weeks to prepare and pack his things, and in June he must report for duty. He was to join the Duke of Wellington's Regiment, nicknamed "the Dukes". The family held a small birthday celebration then Tom packed his suitcase, strapped it to the back of his motorcycle and set off.

To Tom, it felt a bit like heading off on holiday, but when he reached the regiment's base, he soon noticed a few differences between army training and a fun trip away. When Tom arrived, he had to pack everything

Tom in uniform

61

he was wearing into his suitcase and put on a khaki green wool uniform he was given. Tom also had to write a will. A will is a document that tells people what you would like to happen to your possessions in the event of your death. Tom wrote that if he died, he wanted everything he owned to go to his sister Freda. The accommodation wasn't much like a holiday home either. Each new recruit was given a scratchy wool blanket and a thin mattress, set up on the floor of a small tent they had to share. When they weren't in their tent, Tom and the other new recruits were marching, training to fight or pressing their uniform, to keep it looking tiptop.

Be the Best

Army life suited Tom. He didn't mind his uncomfortable bed in his shared tent. He didn't even mind the food, though it wasn't as good as at home. When he was training, he soon noticed that some people at the camp were treated better than others. They had nicer uniforms, smarter boots, fancier food and comfier places to sleep.

These people were officers and Tom decided that he would do whatever it took to become one.

"I DECIDED THAT I'M GOING TO BECOME ONE OF THE BEST."

Captain Sir Tom Moore

Tom knew it wouldn't be easy to reach that rank, but what he didn't know was that he had already sown some of the seeds for success by arriving on his motorcycle. Not long after he arrived at the base, one of the sergeant majors asked to borrow Tom's motorcycle to go and meet a woman for a date. Tom agreed and found that he didn't have to take part in the more difficult marches from that point on.

BRITISH ARMY RANKS

Before reforms in the 1870s, families from the upper and middle land-owning classes could pay to join the British Army at a high rank by buying a commission – a document signed by the king or queen. This meant all of the officers in the army were from the upper classes and that many were not qualified to be there. In World Wars One and Two, while the majority of officers still came from the upper classes, soldiers from less wealthy backgrounds could rise through the ranks by working hard and completing various levels of training successfully and by proving themselves on the battlefield.

Private (second class), Private (first class)	Most junior rank of trained soldier.
Corporal	First levels of officer – without commission.

Sergeant	Commands a group of 7-12 soldiers called a section.
Warrant officer	Warrant officers are the most senior and are responsible for discipline within the unit.
Second Lieutenant	First level of commissioned officer – commands a group of three or four sections called a platoon.
Lieutenant	More experienced platoon commander with additional responsibilities.
Captain	Head, or second in command of a group of platoons called a company.

Major

More experienced head of a company.

Lieutenant colonel

Leader of a battalion – a group of around 1,000 soldiers, consisting of multiple companies.

Colonel

Staff officer in charge of administrative needs of three companies, known as a brigade.

Brigadier

Commander of a brigade in the field.

Major general

Commands a group of three brigades known as a division. A division is made up of around 16,000 soldiers.

Lieutenant general

Commander of two to three divisions called a corps.

General

Commander of an army.

The War in Europe

While Tom was completing his training, war was raging in Europe. After invading Poland in September 1939, Germany set their sights on Scandinavia and in April 1940, crossed the border into Denmark and invaded Norway. In the months of May and June in 1940 the German army invaded Belgium and the Netherlands and moved through France pushing British troops back to the coast. Outnumbered, the British government called for all sea-going vessels to sail across the Channel to rescue more than 300,000 soldiers from the harbour and beaches of Dunkirk, France. Germany had proved themselves a formidable force and they became stronger still when Italy made good on their Axis agreement with Germany and declared war on France and Great Britain on 10 June 1940.

Man in Uniform

On his first weekend leave, Tom returned home to Keighley in his uniform. Most of his family thought he looked very smart and grown up, but one family member didn't like his new look one little bit – his dog, Billy, who barked and wouldn't go near him!

On 31 August 1940, while Tom was at home, he went on a night out to catch up with some friends. At half past ten, when Tom was on his way back to Club Nook, the night air erupted with the loud wail of sirens. Wardens had spotted bombers over Bradford, around fifteen kilometres (nine miles) away. Tom and his friends hurried to find a shelter. The horizon lit up with the blaze of fires, caused by more than one hundred German bombs. In Bradford, more than 10,000 windows were shattered, and one hundred people were injured in the attack. Sadly, one person was killed – but it could easily have been much worse. Scenes like the one in Bradford on 31 August were happening all over the United Kingdom.

THE BLITZ

Between September 1940 and May 1941, the Nazi air force, known as the *Luftwaffe*, dropped thousands of bombs on towns and cities all over the United Kingdom killing an estimated 43,500 people and injuring many more. This was known as the Blitz. The *Luftwaffe* chose cities in the hope of destroying strategic targets such as arms factories and airfields; they also hoped the repeated bombing would destroy morale and lead to a quick surrender from the British. London was bombed more than any other city, but due to its size, many areas escaped devastation. In smaller cities, single air raids wiped out vast areas of the town. Between 14 and 15 November 1940 more than 30,000 bombs were dropped on the city of Coventry, killing 568 people and injuring 850 more. More than one third of the homes in Coventry were damaged beyond repair.

The devastation in Bradford and the continued bombing of cities around the country made Tom even more determined to prove himself when he returned to training. He worked hard, listened to his officers and did everything he could to be useful to his regiment. His efforts didn't go unnoticed. He was soon promoted to corporal and given a pay rise.

Beside the Seaside

Not long after his promotion, Tom and the Dukes moved to another tented encampment in the seaside town of Newquay, Cornwall. In normal times, it was a popular holiday destination – but this was not the time for a holiday. It was the winter of 1940, and the weather was so cold that a bottle of ink in Tom's kit bag froze. Even if the weather had been warm, Cornwall's beaches were off limits to holidaymakers. To prevent a Nazi invasion from the sea, many beaches were barricaded with barbed wire, and some had land mines buried in the sand. Tourist hotels had been turned into army hospitals and tennis courts were used for army drills. Tom and his regiment were in Newquay to patrol the coastline in search of any signs of invasion from mainland Europe.

One of Tom's duties was to guard the camp

at night. Tom had to patrol the perimeter of the camp to make sure no one attempted to break in – and that no one tried to sneak out. One night, while Tom was on guard, a soldier did try to leave the camp. Tom didn't hesitate; he stood in front of the escaping soldier and wouldn't let him pass. The soldier assured Tom that he had a good reason to leave, but Tom stood firm. Tom knew that if it was found out that he let the soldier pass, he could lose his promotion. Even worse than that, if the soldier was a spy leaving the camp to share secrets, the consequences could be disastrous. Tom reported the soldier to his commanding officer. When news spread around the camp the next day, Tom was not very popular, but his commanding officer was impressed. He respected the fact that Tom had put duty, and the safety of the camp, above being popular among his fellow soldiers.

Almost an Officer

The commanding officer recommended Tom for another promotion. Not long after, Tom was sent for training to become an officer. Tom had worked hard to be the best soldier he could be and, in little over six months, he was well on the way to achieving what he had set out to do.

Tom's officer training was split between units in Droitwich, Worcestershire and Heysham, Lancashire. Tom was as determined to do well as ever, but all the time he worried that he would slip up. He thought the army might change its mind and decide Tom Moore wasn't officer material after all. But in spite of his worries, he worked hard, did as he was told and proved that he could be trusted to lead a platoon.

In less than a year, Tom had risen from a humble private to a second lieutenant assigned to the 9th Battalion. So far Tom had done well, but all of his military service had been on bases and camps around England. Soon Tom would have to prove himself much further afield. Where in the world that would be was not for him to decide.

A WORLD WAR

With bombs raining down on Britain's towns and cities, and the German Army's successful occupation of France, just thirty-three kilometres (twenty miles) off the coast, the war felt very close to home. It could have been easy for many in the United Kingdom to forget that Britain and the Allies were involved in a war that affected much of the world.

From the 1600s, European countries, such as Great Britain, sent ships all over the world to claim lands rich in resources such as oil, coal, rubber and cotton, as British territory, whether the people living there liked it or not (most did not). These countries were known as colonies and were ruled by Britain as part of the British Empire.

As well as plans to invade the UK, Germany and the Nazis also wanted to take control of the British territories overseas such as Burma and Malaysia in Asia, and Sudan and Kenya in Africa. The Allies sent troops to protect these countries from invasion. During World War Two, more than 3.5 million soldiers from all over the British Empire volunteered to fight alongside troops from the British mainland.

The War in Africa June 1940–May 1943

Troops from Allied nations fought the Germans and Italians to protect their colonial interests from invasion. Fighting took place in Tunisia, Morocco, Egypt, Algeria and Libya. As well as fighting on the continent, African nations that were part of the British Empire sent troops to Europe and Asia to fight alongside troops from the British mainland.

The War in Asia

World conflict in Asia had loomed over the area since 1931 when the Japanese Imperial Army invaded the region of Manchuria in northeast China. Like the Germans, the Japanese wanted to expand their territory and occupy land rich in resources, such as coal, iron for steel production and oil. Increasing tension between Japan and China eventually led to all-out war. In 1937, Japan launched a full invasion of China and took control of much of its territory. As well as China, Japan had its sights set on Malaya (now Malaysia), Indochina (now Vietnam and Laos) and the Philippines. To put pressure on the Japanese to halt their invasion, Allied nations stopped selling vital resources to Japan, such as oil and steel. The Japanese army needed these resources to continue fighting in China. Despite this, Japan invaded Indochina in 1940 and looked set to continue its offence across the continent.

TOM GOES TO WAR

In August 1941, Tom was promoted to 2nd lieutenant and became a commissioned officer. Life in the army had been good to him, he'd worked hard and made friends too. Tom's best friend was a fellow officer named Philip Thornton from Monmouthshire, Wales. Like Tom, Philip loved nature and the outdoors and, of all the soldiers Tom had met, he was the one he would most like to take home to meet his family at Club Nook.

In the summer of 1941, Tom was given word that he and Philip were being sent to India to protect it from invasion by the Japanese Imperial Army who were advancing through Burma. In August, Tom, Philip and their fellow officers, travelled to Liverpool to board the *Duchess of York*, one of a fleet of ships heading east to India. The journey took eight weeks. Life onboard ship was cramped. To pass the time and take their minds off the constant threat of attack from German U-boats, the men organized talent shows, did regular exercise and took part in boxing championships. As an officer, Tom had to come up with useful ways to keep the men busy, so he taught them all he knew about the workings of engines, something he was very familiar with after the time he had spent in Uncle Billy's workshop.

Voyage to Africa

On the journey, the ship made a number of stops to refuel and to pick up supplies. Tom and the men weren't often allowed to leave the ship on these stop-offs, but when they docked in Cape Town, South Africa, they were given leave to explore. In Cape Town, Tom experienced some of the perks of being an officer. He was taken sightseeing and driven around in a fancy car. Tom was fascinated by Table Mountain, which he could see in the distance. He imagined it to be as smooth as a tennis court on top, but sadly he didn't have time to climb it and find out. Instead, he was whisked off to glamorous parties – opportunities that wouldn't have been available to him as a private – and given a glimpse of a life very different to the one he led with his family in Yorkshire.

India at Last!

On 22 October 1941 the *Duchess of York* arrived in Bombay (now Mumbai). To Tom, who had travelled extensively around England but had only ventured abroad once to Switzerland, Bombay was unlike anywhere he had been to before. It was hot, bustling and filled with colours and fragrances that were unfamiliar to him. From Bombay, Tom travelled 150 kilometres (ninety-three miles) by rail to the Kirkee Royal Artillery Barracks just outside Poona, where he was shown to his quarters. While most of the men were expected to sleep in hot and crowded tents Tom, who was now an officer, was shown to a bungalow, which he shared with three other officers. The bungalow was cool and airy and even had its own attendant to look after the housekeeping and make their meals.

Valentine tank

Once the new arrivals were settled in, it was time for training. The Dukes were to become part of the 50th Indian Tank Brigade. Tom and his men were put to work learning everything they could about fighting in tanks. This was a challenge as many of the men had never driven a car, let alone a tank. Tom's engineering experience meant he was more than up to the job. He was a quick learner and, although he had not driven a tank before, at just twenty years old he was soon teaching soldiers, many older than himself, how to operate and maintain the giant war machines.

Operating a tank was not easy and could not be done alone. Each tank was operated by three men: one to drive it, one to operate the gun and one – the tank commander – who was in charge of giving directions and reloading the gun. Conditions were very cramped, and it was important that the three men trusted one another and got along well. Each member of the team had their own duties but had to be skilled enough to take over from one another if someone was injured.

Tom and his men needed to learn fast. Just over six weeks after Tom arrived in India, the Japanese made a number of moves that would change the course of the war. In need of raw materials such as oil, iron and rubber, the Japanese Imperial Army launched almost simultaneous attacks around the Pacific on 8 December and declared war on the USA and the Allies. Japanese actions in the Pacific proved that they were no longer a force that could be ignored. Hours after the attack on Pearl Harbor, the United Kingdom and the USA declared war on Japan.

REMEMBER, REMEMBER
7 / 8 OF DECEMBER

Japanese pilots drop bombs on a US airbase in Luzon, Philippines, destroying more than one hundred aircraft.

Japanese ground troops march into Thailand from French Indochina (French territory – now Vietnam and Laos). Despite fighting fiercely, the Thai army are forced to surrender in just five hours.

Japanese landing ships supported by fighter planes reach Kota Bharu in Malaya (British territory – now Malaysia) and commence an invasion.

Japanese launch an attack on Hong Kong (British territory), which is forced to surrender by 25 December.

Six squadrons of Japanese bombers attack Singapore (British Territory), killing more than sixty people and injuring 700.

Japanese fighter planes attack Pearl Harbor in Honolulu, Hawaii, USA, destroying 188 US aircraft and damaging more than twenty ships, three beyond repair. More than 2,400 Americans died in the attack.

The bombing of Pearl Harbor took place on 7 December AFTER the attacks on the Philippines, Thailand, Malaya and Singapore on 8 December. This is possible due to the position of the International Date Line.

Rainy Season

The comfortable life at the camp in Kirkee did not last much longer. Tom and his brigade moved to a place called Dhond. Dhond had no nearby towns and was very wet and muddy. As well as the rainy conditions, there were poisonous snakes, biting insects and spiders as big as hands. The toilets consisted of muddy holes in the ground and were infested with flies. The men had to hold their breath when they used them because the stink was so foul.

Tom trained the men to drive tanks in the thick mud and was given his very own tank to command. It was a tradition for a tank commander to give his tank a name. Tom named his Gog after a legendary giant who roamed ancient Britain. But Tom didn't get the chance to take Gog into battle.

Tom's New Job

It was important for the army to have tanks and men with the skills to operate them, but they also needed up-to-date information about the terrain and what to expect when they got there. For this, they needed good communication. Units often used radio, but this could be overheard by the enemy. To make sure messages got through without being intercepted, the army relied on military messengers on motorcycles, called dispatch riders.

Tom was asked to report to his brigadier. Tom's first thought was that he was in some sort of trouble, but the truth was quite the opposite. The army needed more motorcycle dispatch riders and he wanted Tom to become one and teach a team of men the skills they needed to ride too. The brigadier told Tom that he wanted him to set up and run a motorcycle training course. Tom was a skilled engineer and an excellent teacher. This, added to the fact that he knew his way around a motorcycle, showed his commanding officers that he was the man for the job. The brigadier told Tom that it was a matter of great urgency and gave him permission to order whatever he thought he might need from the company store. For Tom, heading up his own motorcycle training course was a dream come true. But as excited as Tom was, he knew it was a big responsibility.

DISPATCH RIDERS

The job of a dispatch rider was to deliver top-secret messages in the shortest time possible. These messages included everything from orders to weather reports, military intelligence to photographs. It was a dangerous job; dispatch riders had to ride alone through war zones and over difficult terrain. Dispatch riders were often given maps that were out of date and were instructed to stay off main roads as much as possible to avoid interception. If they were caught by the enemy, riders were given instructions to destroy their messages by whatever means possible.

Essential kit: as well as their important messages, riders carried a pistol to defend themselves and a toolkit, which contained nuts, bolts, washers, spare inner tubes, spark plugs, and everything needed to fix the motorcycle if it broke down.

Once Tom had everything he needed, he began training British and Indian soldiers how to ride. Many of the soldiers had never ridden a motorcycle before, and those who had had never ridden in such difficult conditions. A lot of the new riders struggled with balancing on two wheels and fell off over and over again, but Tom persevered. It was essential that the riders were well trained because the terrain was some of the most challenging in the world. As well as the mud, there was thick jungle and rocky mountains to contend with. Thankfully, Tom's years of putting his motorcycle through its paces in the field behind his house, then racing over the dales, as well as watching Uncle Billy speed through rivers and up muddy hillsides, meant he was more than up to the task.

Tom gave lessons on how to repair motorcycles, too. He taught the students how to use their tools to take their motorcycles apart and put them back together again, just as he had learned in Uncle Billy's cellar. Once they became dispatch riders, Tom's students would be on their own, carrying messages between posts. If their motorcycles broke down, there would be no one there to help them. In order to make sure both they and their messages made it to their destination safely, riders had to be able fix their motorcycles themselves – fast. Tom needed to teach them as much as he could as quickly as possible, because the Japanese were getting nearer every day.

THE ENEMY DRAWS NEAR

After the attacks in 1941, the Japanese Imperial Army moved through Asia swiftly. Allied troops met them when they arrived in Burma (now Myanmar) in 1942. Both sides fought bravely, but the Allies had underestimated the strength of the Japanese and suffered heavy losses. After fierce fighting, the Japanese won and the Allies were forced to retreat almost 1,600 kilometres (1,000 miles) across the border into India.

The Japanese Army was a fearsome foe. They were trained to be unquestionably loyal to their emperor and to their commanders, and that it was cowardly to surrender under any circumstances. It was their duty to fight bravely to the death.

Tom's regiment was given orders to move too – nearly 1,500 kilometres (900 miles) east to Ranchi. Moving more than 500 men and military vehicles 1,500 kilometres across India was no easy feat. The monsoon season made the journey almost impossible. Heavy rains washed out the roads; many of the vehicles got stuck in the mud and needed to be dug out. The convoy had to stop often to rest and maintain the vehicles.

Tom wasn't able to teach anyone anything about motorcycles on the journey, because he had an even more important job to do. Tom had earned a reputation of being good with maps, so he rode in one of the lead vehicles. Tom put the navigation skills he'd learned in the passenger seat of the Moores' family car to good use by helping to guide the convoy through the jungle.

Tom was so good at navigating that his colonel couldn't believe it. On a particularly difficult leg of the journey, the colonel accused him of being lost and leading the convoy in the wrong direction. Tom, who had known how to read a map since he was a little boy, knew exactly where they were. To prove it, he told the colonel that, according to the map, they would find a mile marker in a bush a little way ahead. The colonel sent someone to check. Tom had been right all along. The colonel was both annoyed and impressed. From then on, whenever he needed to go somewhere, he made sure Tom was his personal driver.

The convoy arrived at the busy camp in Ranchi in July. While it was hot, the camp had the benefit of a nearby lake that the men could swim in to cool off. One of Tom's jobs at the camp was to give the men lectures on Japanese culture, so they could learn more about the people they were fighting. As Tom didn't know much more about the Japanese than the men, he was given a pack of information, which he studied quickly before giving lectures in one of the tents. Tom did his best, but the afternoons in Ranchi were hot and he often noticed soldiers using his talks as an opportunity to take a nap. As well as Tom's lectures, the men underwent training in everything from camouflage to mine clearing to how to steer a tank out of traps.

The regiment was impatient for action having trained for so many months. It wasn't long before some of the men were told that they were going to meet the Japanese in battle. Tom wasn't among those given orders to go, but his good friend Philip Thornton was. Tom wished he could go with him and wished him good luck as he left.

Disaster in Donbaik

The men were sent to place called Donbaik in Myanmar (then called Burma). The terrain in Donbaik was muddy with very steep hills. As well as this the Japanese had constructed bunkers which meant only a few tanks could pass through. It was heavily defended, but army intelligence believed the Japanese had few anti-tank weapons in the region and hoped that with enough support from ground troops, they would prevail. Philip was in command of one of the tanks.

As the men advanced it soon became clear that army intelligence had been wrong. The Japanese had dug deep pits and covered them over to make tank traps. As Philip and the other tanks moved into the area, unable to see the traps, the tanks rolled right into them. Japanese rained heavy fire on the tanks. Of the three tanks from Tom's regiment sent, none returned. When Tom's brigade got the news, they were devastated. Tom wrote to his friend Philip's parents at home to tell them what a good friend Philip had been and how popular he was among the men.

Not long after this, Tom was sent for further navigational training near Calcutta. While he was there, he picked up more than new knowledge and encountered an enemy even more deadly than the Japanese. He began to feel very ill on his way back to camp and had to stop at a hotel. It turned out Tom had caught a bad case of dengue fever.

FIGHTING AN UNSEEN ENEMY

In India and Burma, the wet, unsanitary conditions and abundance of insects and parasites meant soldiers were much more likely to die from disease than be killed by the Japanese Army.

DENGUE FEVER

Dengue is a virus transmitted by mosquitoes. Symptoms can appear up to ten days after being bitten by an infected mosquito. Symptoms of dengue fever include headache, vomiting, fever and a rash. Severe dengue fever can cause severe bleeding and death.

MALARIA

Malaria is caused by a parasite transmitted by mosquitoes. Symptoms include headache, fever, shivering, sweating, vomiting and diarrhoea. Severe malaria can cause major organs in the body to fail which may lead to coma and death.

SCRUB TYPHUS (TSUTSUGAMUSHI DISEASE)

Scrub typhus is a bacterial disease transmitted by chigger mites. Symptoms include a dark scab around the area of the bite, headache, high fever, muscle pain, confusion and a rash. If left untreated scrub typhus can be fatal. Scrub typhus can be treated with antibiotics.

JUNGLE ROT

Jungle rot is a fungal infection caused by prolonged wetness. Symptoms include swelling, tingling and numbness. Severe jungle rot can lead to open sores, severe bacterial infection and death.

Tom was fortunate. Despite feeling very ill and losing a lot of weight, he made a full recovery and was able to return to his post. But others were not so lucky. In 1943, for every one casualty injured in battle, 120 were evacuated due to sickness.

On the Mend and On the Move

··

When Tom recovered, he returned to his post in Ranchi. From there, the regiment moved to Poona (Pune) and then 2,500 kilometres (1,500 miles) east to Chittagong (Chattogram is its name now), Bangladesh. Tom and his men were sent to Chittagong to defend an important port and airbase from Japanese attack. The conditions were some of the worst Tom had experienced. All of the men slept in tents deep within the dense jungle. With the terrible living situation, the constant threat of an enemy attack, as well as sickness, morale among the troops was at an all-time low. The regiment were also aware that, back home, most of the government's attention and resources was directed towards the fighting in Europe. To help boost the spirits of the soldiers and remind them that they were not forgotten, the commanders had just the remedy – the Entertainment National Service Association (ENSA).

While Tom was in Chittagong he saw a beautiful woman emerge from the dense forest accompanied by Lord Mountbatten himself. The woman was Vera Lynn. Vera chatted with the men before she sang for them, just as she had for so many others.

Dame Vera Lynn with troops

ENTERTAINMENTS NATIONAL SERVICE ASSOCIATION (ENSA)

ENSA was established in 1939 to provide entertainment for the troops serving overseas. ENSA worked with the army, navy and air force to send talented performers to entertain the troops wherever they were stationed. Even though many of the performers were famous actors and singers, they weren't given special treatment. They weren't expected to fight, but they stayed in the same horrible conditions, ate the same rations and travelled in the same trucks and planes as the soldiers.

Vera Lynn was a popular singer who played outdoor concerts for troops in India, Burma and Egypt. Her most famous songs from that time were **"We'll Meet Again"** and **"The White Cliffs of Dover"**. For her work with ENSA she was nicknamed the "forces sweetheart" because she reminded the men of home and the people they loved, who missed them and waited for them to come back.

"BURMA WAS A SPECIAL TIME FOR ME AND ONE THAT I WILL NEVER FORGET. I WAS WELL PROTECTED BY ALL THE BOYS AND NEVER FELT FRIGHTENED. IT WAS SO GOOD TO HELP THEM FEEL THAT THEY WERE NOT SO FAR AWAY FROM HOME."

Dame Vera Lynn

Vera Lynn's appearance in the jungle boosted the regiment's morale, but it didn't last long. Soon after Vera Lynn had left, Tom's regiment was ordered into Burma, to a place called Arakan.

On to Arakan

In early 1944, Tom travelled to Arakan to face some of the fiercest fighting in World War Two. After years of training, it was the time to put all of his skills into action. The fighting was fierce as Tom and his company moved further into Burma. They fought in all different terrain, meeting the enemy wherever they encountered them whether in rice fields or deep within the jungle. As they pushed on, their way was often blocked by water; the bridges washed out by heavy rains or destroyed by the enemy. When this happened, Tom and his unit had to dig deep ditches in which to conceal themselves and send a dispatch rider to fetch the army engineers. When the engineers arrived, they swiftly constructed temporary crossings so Tom and his men could proceed. British, American and Indian troops, as well as troops from all over the British Empire, fought side by side to push back the Japanese. Tom and his unit were regularly under fire and battles often involved hand to hand combat.

Sunset offered no rest for the tired soldiers, as the Japanese often attacked at night. These kinds of attacks were especially difficult for the British troops, because not only were they unable to see where the enemy was, but also they couldn't use their tanks safely in the dark. Tank commanders drove their tanks away from the front before nightfall and only returned when they had received an "all clear" message from the front, letting them know the night-time fighting was over. As a skilled infantry liaison officer, it was Tom's job to carry messages between the posts. During the night, Tom remained with the soldiers at the front, fighting off any enemy attack. If all was clear the next morning, armed only with a pistol, Tom rode through the jungle alone, back to where

Sikh soldier

the tanks were stationed. He knew that, at any moment, he could be picked off by an enemy sniper or arrive at a camp already overrun by the Japanese.

Help From Above

By 1944, things were improving. The Allied soldiers on the ground were no longer alone. The Allied air force had taken control of the skies above Burma and were able to deliver supplies, provide surveillance and give armed support. This was just what the British troops needed to make real progress against the Japanese, pushing them further and further back.

Tom fought bravely at Arakan and was an excellent infantry liaison officer. His achievements didn't go unnoticed. Tom's commanding officers were pleased with how he had performed and recommended him for a promotion. Tom was promoted to captain on 11 October 1944.

BACK TO BLIGHTY

Tom and his company fought hard and were making progress. To help them on their way, the British Army ordered a number of new tanks, named Churchill tanks after the prime minister of the time, Winston Churchill. But before these new tanks were taken into battle, the army needed to make sure soldiers knew how to use them. For this they needed Tom. A talented engineer and excellent teacher, Tom's commanding officers ordered him to go back to England. When he arrived, his orders were to familiarize himself with the new Churchill tanks, and learn how to operate and repair them as quickly as he could, so that he could return to Burma and teach the men how best to use them in the fight against the Japanese Imperial Army. Tom was disappointed to be sent home, however important the job. As much as he longed to see his family, he wanted to stay to finish what he had started in Burma and help win the Battle of Arakan. But the decision had been made and, once again, Tom went where the army felt his skills were most needed.

The army thought his skills were needed so urgently that, instead of travelling by ship as he had before, in March 1945 Tom flew onboard an army aircraft. It was much faster than travelling by boat, even though the plane made a few stops. He arrived in England six days later. It was his first time on British soil in almost four years and, although it was spring, it seemed cold and overcast in comparison to India.

Tom travelled to Bovington, Dorset, where was to work as an instructor at the Armoured Fighting Vehicle School. The morning after he arrived, he called his mother and promised to visit her as soon as he was given leave.

Happy Homecoming

When Tom finally got the chance to go home to visit his family, his father was waiting for him at the station. He was relieved and delighted to see his son return home safely. Back at the house, Tom was treated like a hero. Tom's family didn't usually like to make a fuss, but for Tom's return, the Moores hoisted a Union Jack up the flagpole at Club Nook.

That evening, Tom got something he had been missing the whole time he had been away – a meal cooked by his mother. For Tom's homecoming, his mother pooled all the family rations and called in favours from the farmers nearby to make Tom his favourite meal of roast beef and Yorkshire puddings, and a yummy dessert. But even though it was his first visit home in years, he didn't get to stay long. Tom had to report back to camp within thirty-six hours.

Back at the Bovington Armoured Fighting Vehicle School, Tom familiarized himself with the Churchill tank quickly. He was impressed with the new tank; it had thicker armour and tracks that were better suited to the difficult terrain in Burma. Tom hoped that he would soon get to share his new knowledge with his friends still fighting in Burma, but he wasn't sure he would get the chance.

Victory in Europe

After successive Allied victories in Europe, two months after Tom's return, Germany surrendered. Victory in Europe was declared on 8 May 1945. This marked the end of the war in Europe. Everyone at Tom's camp was given a day off work and people all over the country celebrated the momentous news.

Tom did not take part in the celebrations. While he was pleased the war in Europe was over, he worried about his comrades still fighting and dying in Asia and was determined to work as hard as he could in order to be able to join them as soon as possible. Tom's hard work had unexpected consequences. The commanding officers at the camp in Bovington were so impressed with his skills that they wanted him to stay on and train men there.

Tom stayed on at the camp, but he followed the news of the conflict in Burma and celebrated every victory. Despite the success of Allied forces and sustained air attacks of Japanese cities, the Japanese refused to surrender. They were prepared to fight to the very end. That end came when the United States Air Force dropped atomic bombs on the cities of Hiroshima on 6 August 1945 and Nagasaki on 9 August. The devastation caused by the bombs left the Japanese Emperor little choice but to surrender, which he did on 15 August 1945.

HIROSHIMA AND NAGASAKI

On 6 August 1945 a US B-29 Bomber dropped a 16-kiloton bomb which exploded 580 metres (1,900 feet) above the ground, killing an estimated 80,000 civilians instantly and more than 50,000 others as a result of long-term radiation caused by the bomb. Three days later, this was followed by the dropping of a second 21-kiloton bomb on the city of Nagasaki, killing more than 50,000 people.

A 16-kiloton bomb means that it was as powerful as a bomb made from 16,000 tons of

Trinitrotoluene (TNT) – the explosive used to manufacture standard bombs.

An atomic bomb is a bomb which gets its power by splitting apart the nucleus of an atom. Atoms are held together by very strong forces and splitting them apart releases huge amounts of energy – enough to destroy entire cities. Atomic bombs are lethal not only when they explode, but for a long time afterwards because they release huge amounts of radioactive material. Radioactive material is material that gives off atomic radiation. Radiation is energy that moves from one place to another. Some radiation is harmless, such as light, and sound; atomic radiation is very dangerous as it can cause serious damage to the cells of living things. When first released radioactive material can cause serious burns, but once in the environment, radioactive material can cause cancer.

Victory over Japan

On 15 August 1945, US President Harry Truman declared victory over Japan. Shortly after, British Prime Minister Clement Attlee announced the news to the people of Great Britain. Towns and cities across the country erupted in celebration. In contrast to the dark days of the blackout, floodlights shone on public buildings and people were given a two-day holiday as a reward for all they had sacrificed during the conflict. This time, Tom joined in too.

For Tom, and for so many others, victory over Japan meant that their time in the armed forces could soon come to an end. Tom wasn't sure at first if he wanted to leave the army. Despite the harsh conditions he experienced in Burma, army life suited him, and he'd enjoyed his time with the regiment. He had also proven himself to be an excellent soldier and risen quickly through the ranks. The army awarded Tom medals for his service – the 1939–1945 Star, the Burma Star, the Defence Medal and the War Medal. Tom's medals were sent to him at home.

Tom's medals

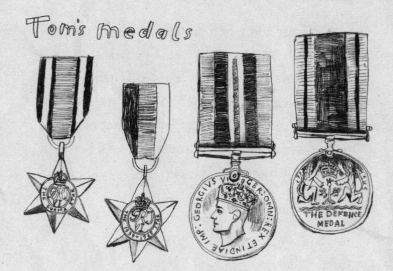

As much as Tom wanted to stay in the army, he didn't feel like he could make that choice. He had responsibilities at home. Tom's father, Wilfred, was getting older and the building business started by his grandfather many years ago was struggling. The war was tough on the construction industry. All materials were heavily rationed, and builders had to fight for approval for any new construction, which could take weeks. Materials could be purchased on the black market, but this was illegal and very expensive, and few people had the money to be able to afford it. To keep the business afloat,

Tom's father had taken on smaller projects, such as repairing buildings that were damaged in the bombings and adding extensions, but it hadn't been enough. While Tom had liked the idea of staying in the army, he knew his father needed him more. He decided to home to work at what was now W. Moore and Son.

INSPIRING

NEW BEGINNINGS

While it wasn't his first choice, there was a lot to like about living at home again. In the army, he had missed his mother's cooking and being with his family. Now, he had his old room back and things at Club Nook were a lot like they had always been. But life in Riddlesden wasn't the same as it had been when Tom left. Rationing was still in force and Tom found he need a coupon for almost anything he might want, from shoes to petrol.

Tom wasn't the same either. When he left, he had been a boy, but now he was a twenty-five-year-old man who had lived through and fought in a war. But Tom made the best of it. He was determined to work hard and build the family business up to what it had been when his grandfather Thomas had been in charge. He and his father had always been good friends and even though his father's deafness made it hard to talk, they had always had nice times with each other and found they worked together very well.

But Tom still felt lonely. Like many servicemen and women returning from the war, Tom found that it was difficult to talk to his family about his experiences. This was hard for Tom. He missed his friends in the army and the strong bond they all shared. He wanted to know how they were all doing and what coming home was like for them.

In 1947, Tom went to a reunion with his fellow officers in London. For Tom, it was an opportunity to be around people who understood and experienced many of the same things as he had during the war. But Tom wanted to find out how everyone in his regiment was doing, too, so he organized a reunion for all of the men in the Duke of Wellington's regiment, not just the officers. It was hard work putting the event together. He had to book a venue, organize food and drink and send out more than 120 invitations. The effort was worth it and he and the men and had a wonderful time being together again. It was so wonderful, in fact, that Tom would organize a similar event every year for the next sixty-five years.

Wedding Bells

One of the good things about moving back home was meeting up with old friends. One of Tom's friends, Brian Booth, had fought in France. Tom was happy to meet up with him again, especially when Brian's girlfriend, Pat, brought along a friend named Billie. Tom liked Billie immediately, not only because she was friendly and pretty, but also because Billy had always been a special name to him. Tom began to see a lot of Billie and even took her home to meet his parents at Club Nook. The pair grew close and Tom asked Billie to be his wife. In 1949, Tom and Billie married in a small ceremony in Esholt, West Yorkshire.

Tom was excited to start a new life with his beautiful bride, but his father wasn't so sure about Billie, or about his son getting married. He had wanted the family to stay together. But Tom didn't move far. He and Billie lived close by so that Tom could work for the family business.

Tom had everything he thought he wanted, a wife and a good job close to his family, but he wasn't happy. While they were very much in love when they married, Tom and Billie's love didn't last. After the wedding they found they didn't have much in common. Tom loved travelling and the outdoors and Billie didn't care for either. She loved pop music and staying close to home. Tom and Billie did everything they could to make their marriage a happy one, but nothing seemed to work. Tom and Billie argued, and Tom felt lonely because he didn't feel like he could talk to anyone about their problem, so they carried on unhappily for many years.

Back on the Bike

← Trophy

Tom and his motorbike

To take his mind off his home life, Tom threw himself into an old hobby. He took up motorbike racing again, taking part in trials all over the north of England. It reminded Tom of the happy days he had shared with his uncle and of the thrill of driving through India and Burma. On a motorcycle, Tom felt free.

As well as motorcycle racing, Tom wanted to help his community. To do this he joined his local Round Table. The Round Table was a social club for young men between the ages of eighteen and forty-five years old. It was a place for these men to make friends, share ideas and work together to improve their local community. This was perfect for Tom, who had enjoyed the friendship and camaraderie he felt during the war. Tom threw himself into the organization and was soon elected chairman.

Finding his Fundraising Skills

While working with the Round Table, Tom got his first taste of raising money for causes close to his heart. He found that he was good at it.

Growing up, Tom saw how his father's disability had affected his life and kept him from meeting new people. Tom wanted to give people who were isolated, either through disability or because they lived alone, a place where they could meet and connect with others, and hopefully have a good time. Tom and the Round Table raised money by holding events such as shows and treasure hunts, and by asking for support from local businesses. Eventually they were able to set up a club, provide transportation and even buy a holiday cottage where members of the community who had disabilities could stay with a carer.

Rock Bottom

Unfortunately, the family's building business was not as successful at making money. Tom and his father worked hard and did everything they could to keep it afloat. Wilfred even sold their beloved house, Club Nook, and moved to a smaller house to put money into the business, but it was not enough. Despite all of Tom and his father's efforts, in February 1959 W. Moore and

Son closed for good. Tom was devastated that he had not been able to save the company his grandfather had started and made so successful. As well as this, he was also out of a job. Tom didn't know what he was going to do.

Thankfully, Tom's friend Brian gave him some work at the quarry he ran with his father, ten miles from Skipton in Yorkshire. A quarry is a large pit where stone is taken from the ground to be used for building. Tom started at the bottom, working with the big machines that crushed the rock. Tom had always enjoyed working with machines, so although the work wasn't well paid, it suited him. Tom eventually worked with explosives too, blasting the rock from out of the ground in the quarry. It was hard work, and although Tom enjoyed it, he knew he wanted to do something more. In the army, Tom had worked his way up from private to captain, but at the quarry there wasn't a better job for him to progress to.

Unsatisfied with his job at the quarry, when Tom heard about a job selling magazine subscriptions, he jumped at the chance. Tom had always been good with people and selling door to door meant he would be able to travel independently, just as he had during his apprenticeship. The amount of money Tom earned at his new job was based on commission, which meant the more magazine subscriptions he sold, the more money he made and the better he would do in the company. This was ideal for someone who was ambitious like Tom. But Tom soon discovered that he didn't like what he was selling. When Tom was out on a sales call, he could often tell that the people he was trying to sell to didn't have money spare to spend on magazines. Tom was a natural salesman but felt bad about persuading people to buy things they couldn't afford. Luckily on one of Tom's calls, his salesmanship caught the eye of someone who thought they could use Tom's talents selling other products. These were products that Tom knew well and had first-hand experience of using himself – building materials.

Building a Future

The company was called Nuralite and sold roofing materials. Tom thought that they were excellent products and he found them easy to sell because he believed in them. The job was well paid and came with a car.

His new job meant he and Billie needed to move to Manchester to be closer to his work. Billie struggled with the move. She had liked living in Yorkshire near her family and missed them very much. While Tom and Billie were unhappy at home, Tom was very happy at work. He was an excellent salesman and before long moved to a better paid position at a different company which was based 290 kilometres (180 miles) away in Hemel Hempstead. It was a long drive from Manchester, but for Tom it was worth it. Billie, however, did not like being left alone. Tom did his best to make sure he wasn't away for long. When Tom got yet another job, they moved again to Leeds so that Tom could be home more, but it wasn't enough to save their marriage.

After eighteen years together, Tom and Billie decided to separate in 1967. Tom was unhappy about how things had worked out, but it was time to move on with his life.

Pleasant Company

Tom didn't realize that to move forward he would have to move back – to Nuralite, the company where he had sold roofing materials. Tom had done well since leaving Nuralite. He'd worked at lots of different companies and with each new job he had been promoted, offered a higher salary and given the use of a better car. But Tom had been happy at Nuralite, so when he saw they had an opening for a sales manager, Tom went for it. Nuralite were happy to have him back and Tom was more than happy to be there. Nuralite's main office was based in Gravesend, Kent, and it was there that Tom met a friendly office manager named Pamela. As a sales manager, Tom didn't need to be at the main office except for meetings, but he found that he wanted to be there as often as he could. Tom eventually asked Pamela out on a date, and she agreed.

Tom and Pamela liked each other right away. They went out for lunches and dinners, took trips to the theatre and even went away on holiday together. Tom was smitten but he didn't think it was appropriate to have a relationship with someone he worked with and so, rather than say goodbye to Pamela, he said goodbye to Nuralite again to work for a concrete manufacturer named Cawood, Wharton & Co. After a whirlwind romance, Tom and Pamela married in January 1968.

HAPPY FAMILY

The happy couple moved in with her parents in Gravesend, Kent and in August 1968 were joined by a beautiful baby girl. Tom and Pamela named their daughter Lucy. Tom couldn't believe that after being so unhappy for so long his heart – and his house – was filled with love. But the house was getting a bit crowded. Thankfully Tom was doing well at work and was soon promoted to a better position. Tom used his salary to borrow money from the bank to buy the house from Pamela's parents and help them to buy a smaller house nearby. Pamela was delighted. She loved living in Gravesend and now she wouldn't even have to leave her childhood home.

Concrete Plans

When Tom moved to Cawood Concrete, he took the job as sales manager, but with his civil engineering experience from his early apprenticeship and building-trade knowledge gathered from managing the family company, Tom soon proved he could be even more use to the company. Tom was promoted to managing director of one of the plants, where they made concrete. The owners of the company hoped Tom's experience would help them to make the business more profitable. Tom did just that. Soon after starting, Tom realized the business would sell far more if they cut their prices; he also made the plant work more efficiently by allowing the employees to earn more money by working longer shifts. Soon the plant was working twenty-four hours a day, and the company was making more money than it ever had before.

The plant wasn't the only thing working twenty-four hours. When he wasn't at work, Tom was a devoted father and wanted to spend as much time with his little girl as he could. Pamela looked after baby Lucy when Tom was at the plant, but when he came home he was the one Lucy came to. Unlike many fathers in the 1960s, Tom changed nappies, read stories and was the one Lucy called out for whenever she had bad dreams in the night.

Having been so close to his grandparents when he was a boy, Tom couldn't wait to introduce his little girl to her grandfather and her aunt, Freda. Wilfred was delighted to meet his new granddaughter and very proud of his son and all he had achieved.

A Sad Call

Sadly, Lucy didn't get to spend much time with Grandfather Wilfred, because in May 1970, Tom got a call from his sister: their father was dying. Tom drove to their home as soon as he could, but sadly he was too late to say goodbye. Wilfred Moore died aged eighty-five. He was laid to rest next to his wife, Bella, in Morton Cemetery, Riddlesden. Tom was very sad but was glad that his father had got the chance to see him as a happily married man and meet his first grandchild. Tom liked to visit his parents at the cemetery for many years after they died, to let them know how his life was going.

The Moores' sadness lifted a little later that year, when their daughter Hannah was born. Their family was now complete. Tom sometimes worried that he was older than a lot of Hannah and Lucy's friends' dads who were in their twenties and thirties, while he was in his fifties. Some people even thought he was their grandad instead of their dad – but it didn't bother him too much. He felt very fit and healthy and did everything he could to be the best dad possible and give his daughters a childhood like the one he had, filled with fresh air and outdoor adventures.

He encouraged them to climb as high as they liked in the trees and put them to work in the garden planting and mowing. Tom taught them to cook, just like his mother and grandmother had taught him. The house was full of animals, including pet guinea pigs, rabbits, a cat and a dog named Nero. Tom didn't have much time for sickness or drama. He felt his little girls should be able to get up and get on with things, just as his parents thought he should when he was a boy.

When Tom and Freda were little, Wilfred hadn't believed in buying them toys. He'd bought them tools instead and helped them learn how to make things for themselves. Tom wanted the same for his girls. While other children were given teddy bears and doll's houses, Tom gave his girls tools. He shared with them all the things he had enjoyed growing up. He taught them all about engines and showed them how to fix things. He made sure they learned how to navigate too, just as he had for his father and mother in the Moores' first family car.

Tom loved to take his family on holiday in the car, but his family went a bit further afield than he had as a boy, driving to France, Italy and Spain. Sometimes they even towed a caravan. Tom used his experience leading manoeuvres in India and Burma to run these holidays like a military operation – but luckily for his wife and children, they were much more fun. Tom and the girls planned the routes with meticulous attention to detail and before they left, Tom checked the packing list on his clipboard.

Now well into his fifties, Tom may have thought his racing days were over, but his skills were still much needed by his daughters, who regularly missed their buses to school or college. Tom would jump in the car with the girls and race to catch up with the bus to make sure they could climb aboard at one of the next stops.

First Five Minutes of Fame

Life for Tom was very settled, but that didn't mean he stopped wanting to try new things. In 1983, Tom applied to appear on a television quiz programme called *Blankety Blank*. *Blankety Blank* was presented by the then king of Saturday night TV, Sir Terry Wogan. Tom was delighted

when he received a letter inviting him to be a contestant. Tom jumped at the chance; not only would it be fun, but he would meet celebrity guests and stand a chance of winning real prizes. Unfortunately for Tom, he didn't win, but he had a great time filming and seeing behind the scenes of a television show. He was particularly fascinated with the revolving set. When he'd watched the show at home, he had thought the set was powered by a piece of high-tech machinery. He was disappointed to discover, however, that it was operated with an enormous crank that needed two men to turn it.

As happy as Tom was in his home life, times were hard for many people living in the United Kingdom in the 1980s.

The Early 1980s

The 1980s was a period of change for the United Kingdom. Before 1980, the UK produced lots of different things and sold them to countries all over the world, but this was starting to change. Companies found that it was cheaper to buy things such as coal, steel and other manufactured goods from other countries. This meant lots of people who worked in those industries lost their jobs. In 1979, one in twenty adults was unable to find work, a number which rose to more than one in ten by 1982. Without work, people struggled to pay their rent and feed their families.

Many people in the UK were angry with the government and thought it should do more to help. To get the government's attention, workers went on strike and protested in the streets.

Risky Business

In 1983, the concrete plant Tom was managing was bought by a bigger company. This company already made their own materials, so they didn't need Tom's plant to make concrete any more. They wanted to shut it down, leaving Tom and all of the workers at the plant without a job. Tom didn't want this to happen. He felt that the concrete plant could be profitable with the right management, so he came up with a plan.

Tom invested his own money, plus some

money he borrowed from the bank, and convinced the other managers of the company to do the same. Together, they bought the concrete plant. In return, the managers and Tom would get a share of the profits. It was a risk, but Tom was sure he could make it work. They renamed the company March Concrete. Under Tom and the other managers' direction, the company went from strength to strength. The workers at the plant kept their jobs and the managers saw a good return on their investment.

Four years after buying the company, another even bigger company offered to buy it for much more than Tom and the other investors paid for it. They agreed to sell on one condition: that the new company would keep on all of the plant's workers. The buyer agreed. Tom was delighted that his plan had worked. After working hard for so many years, Tom had enough money to retire comfortably, knowing he had protected his workers from losing their jobs.

A LONG GOODBYE

Tom had worked for over fifty years – he'd been a civil engineering apprentice, a soldier, a builder, a quarry labourer, then worked his way up as a salesman for multiple companies. Eventually, he had become the manager and part-owner of a successful concrete plant. Tom was sixty-seven years old and ready to retire from work, but he wasn't ready to retire from adventures.

Tom had always worked very hard, and he and Pamela hadn't had as much time together as they would have liked. Now Tom had retired, they had more time to travel, enjoy each other's company and grow old together. Tom and Pamela bought a villa in Burgos, Spain and moved in in 1989. Hannah moved with them, as well as their dog Nero and their cat Whiskey. Lucy was married and working for an airline and Hannah was starting a career in sales.

Tom and Pamela were very happy. They enjoyed their new villa, the warm weather, the food and the chance to learn a new language. They travelled all over the country. They were happy, but as they spent more time together, Tom started to notice small changes in Pamela's behaviour. Tom hoped it was nothing, but he thought Pamela seemed less confident than before. He noticed that she talked about people following her and watching what she was doing, when Tom could see there was no one there. Tom hoped more time together would help, but if she needed extra care, then he was sure they would find it. It turned out that at that time in Spain, medical assistance wasn't found as easily as Tom would have liked.

One day, Pamela was out with Hannah when Tom had an accident – he walked through the glass of the patio doors to their villa. The glass smashed and cut Tom so badly that he had to go to hospital. At the hospital, Tom found out he would need surgery to stop the bleeding – but he would have to pay for it first. Tom was shocked. He was used to all of his health emergencies being taken care of by the NHS.

WHAT IS THE NHS?

The NHS stands for the National Health Service. The UK government launched the NHS in 1948. The purpose of the NHS is to provide medical care to people regardless of how much money they have. NHS hospitals and clinics treat around 1.4 million patients every day. The NHS treats patients at no cost, but that does not mean it is free. The NHS is paid for by taxes collected by the government. The government collects taxes from adults in the UK and uses some of that money to fund the NHS. The UK government runs the NHS in England. The health services in Scotland, Wales and Northern Ireland are run by their own governments. Before the NHS, people who needed a doctor or to go to hospital had to pay. This could be very expensive, which meant people who did not have much money were not able to afford the care they needed and had to rely on hospitals run by local charities.

Tom made a full recovery, but Pamela wasn't getting any better. In 1993, Tom felt it was time for him and Pamela to move back to England. Lucy lived there with her husband, and Hannah wanted to move to London. Tom bought a house in Gravesend, Kent where they could be close to family and Pamela could get the care she needed.

Back to Blighty, Again

Due to travel restrictions on animals at the time, Tom's dog Nero and cat Whiskey had to stay in quarantine for six months. This was because UK customs wanted to make sure the animals weren't bringing any diseases found on mainland Europe to the UK. Neither animal liked it very much and Tom was very sad whenever he visited them.

When their quarantine was complete, the pets joined Tom and Pamela in Gravesend, but Nero was now quite old, and it wasn't long until he had to be put down. Tom was devastated. Nero had been a good friend, just as his dog Billy had been when he was a boy. Tom didn't think he wanted another dog, but Pamela insisted, and they got a new puppy they named Harry. Although Tom hadn't been sure about getting a new dog, he ended up loving Harry very much and was grateful for his company over the next years.

Part of Tom hoped that when Pamela returned to England she would return to her old self, but she didn't. Instead, she started getting worse. Pamela was beginning to forget things and Tom couldn't leave her alone in the house in case she accidentally did something to hurt herself, such as leave the gas on. Pamela also imagined she was talking to people who weren't there. Tom was worried, so he went to see his GP to ask what they could do to help. The doctor signed them up with a health visitor who visited Tom and Pamela regularly to see how she was doing. Thankfully, Pamela wasn't really aware of what was happening to her, but for Tom life became increasingly lonely, as he wasn't able to leave the house and spent most of his time taking care of his wife. The doctors weren't sure exactly what was causing Pamela to behave the way she was, but believed she was suffering from something called dementia.

DEMENTIA

Dementia is not a single disease, but is the name given to a number of different conditions that cause nerve cells in the brain, called neurons, to stop communicating with each other properly. This makes it difficult to think, remember and understand things. Dementia can stop people from being able to concentrate, solve problems and manage their emotions. Today, there are more than 850,000 people living with dementia in the United Kingdom. Dementia usually affects people over the age of sixty-five, with one in six people over the age of the eighty living with the condition.

Tom hoped to be able to care for Pamela at home, but at eighty years old it was hard for him to manage. As well as forgetting things, Pamela would become confused and leave the house in the night. Tom had to drive around the streets trying to find her, worrying that she might not be able to find her way home or might step into traffic.

After two years of caring for Pamela himself, Tom came to terms with the fact he needed help, so he went to see the GP again. The doctor suggested that Pamela be admitted to a home run by the NHS that specialized in caring for people suffering with dementia. Tom hoped that after he'd had a bit of a rest he would be able to bring her home, but her condition got worse to the point where it wouldn't be safe for her to return. Tom didn't like to be away from Pamela, but knew she was getting the best care possible. As Pamela's condition worsened, she needed to move to different care facilities. When one home closed, Pamela was moved to a private care facility. Private care was very expensive, especially for someone who needed to be looked after twenty-four hours a day. Tom worried about how he would be able to afford it, but thankfully the NHS covered the cost of Pamela's care until she was moved to another NHS facility.

Tender Loving Care

Tom was relieved to be able to rely on the NHS. He was also grateful to all of the staff who took care of Pamela and the other residents in the home. Tom knew how difficult care work could be and how much work the staff had to do, with so many residents. To help out, Tom visited Pamela every day. When Tom was caring for Pamela at home, he had become very lonely, but when Pamela moved into the care facility, he had lots of people to talk to. Tom got to know Pamela's nurses and liked to talk with them. Tom also made friends with the families of other residents, who understood what he and Pamela had been through. Though Tom now had friends to talk to, it was still a very sad time. Pamela was getting worse and remembering less and less of their time together. There were days when she wasn't able to talk at all.

In 2006, Tom got some very sad news. After fourteen years of suffering with dementia, Pamela had died. Tom was at his daughter Lucy's house when he found out. Tom knew he had done everything he could to care for Pamela and let her know she was loved, but he was sad he hadn't been with his wife to say a final goodbye.

At Pamela's funeral, Tom requested the song "We'll Meet Again", sung by Dame Vera Lynn who he had met in the jungle more than sixty years earlier. Tom hoped that one day he and Pamela would be together again.

Tom missed Pamela very much. Caring for her and visiting her had taken up nearly all of his time for more than ten years, and now she was gone. Tom wasn't sure what he was going to do next, but he knew Pamela would want him to make the most of the time he had left, even if she couldn't be by his side.

TRAVELLING BACK IN TIME

At eighty-six years old, Tom did not look like a young man on the outside, but he felt like one on the inside. He was fit and healthy and very independent. Tom had lived a life filled with challenges and adventures and he was ready for more, but first he wanted to revisit the some of the places he had served during the war.

Tom booked a trip to India. Many of the names of the places he had served as a member of the Duke of Wellington's Regiment had changed. Bombay was now Mumbai. When Tom was in India during the war, India was still ruled by the British.

India after the War

Before war broke out in 1939, many people in India wished to be independent from British rule. These people were led by activists such as

Mahatma Gandhi. Gandhi believed the British exploited Indian people and often treated them cruelly. Gandhi organized peaceful protests against the British and encouraged followers not to cooperate with any aspect of British life including attending schools, paying taxes and appearing in courts of law.

Mahatma Gandhi

Fearing an uprising during World War Two, the British imprisoned Gandhi. The Indian army fought bravely against the Japanese alongside the British and Allied soldiers, in spite of the desire held by many for independence from British rule. After the Allied victory, leaders in India, including Gandhi, continued their campaign. India won independence in 1947 but the land was partitioned into two separate nations: a Hindu nation, India, and a Muslim nation, Pakistan. This caused fierce fighting.

Soon after India won independence the Indian government began to change the names of their towns and cities to what they were called in local languages such as Hindi and Bengali, rather than what they were named by British colonizers. A process that continues to this day.

Old Friends

In 2007, Tom organized a reunion with members of the Duke of Wellington's Regiment. It was a special reunion because it was their sixtieth. For

Yorkshire regiment badge

sixty years, Tom had worked hard to set up these reunions, which were so important to the soldiers who had served together. It was a chance for them to get together and remember what they had been through so many years ago. It gave them an opportunity to talk about their wartime experiences with the only other people who could really understand. Without Tom's commitment, the reunions would never have happened. To thank Tom for all of his hard work over the years, the regiment presented him with a statue of two soldiers. The statue was engraved with Tom's name and a message to say thank you. Over the years, fewer and fewer members of the regiment were able to attend. At the sixtieth celebration, only three members including Tom could come.

Full-time Grandad

In 2007, Hannah told her father that she and her husband, Colin, were moving to Bedfordshire. They wanted to find a house that would suit Tom too, because they wanted him to move in with them. Tom was delighted. He went with Hannah and Colin to look for a suitable place to live and found a house in a village called Marston Moretaine. It was a large house with a big garden. When the sale was complete, Tom and his dog Harry moved in with Hannah, Colin, their son, Benjie, and their new baby girl, Georgia. Tom loved living with Hannah and her family. Tom had loved being a hands-on father to his two girls, and now he could enjoy being a full-time grandfather. He hoped he could be as good a grandparent as his were to him.

Though Tom had moved in with Hannah, he was still very independent. He had lived on his own for a long time and he knew how he liked things to be done. Tom did all his own shopping and cooking and took charge of the house's large garden, racing around it on his very own ride-on mower. The house had a greenhouse, where he attempted to grow tomatoes, and a shed, which he transformed into what the family called "Grandad's Fix-it Shop".

As much as Tom liked tending to his garden, he liked spending time with his grandchildren even more. While Pamela was ill, Tom had not been able to spend as much time with his grandchildren as he would have liked, but now he shared a house with two of them. Tom told Georgia and Benjie stories from when he was growing up and showed them his old camera, along with old things that had belonged to his mother and father. When Benjie got home from school he would chat with his grandad for hours. And whenever Georgia or Benjie broke any of their sports equipment, Tom would mend it with superglue. Tom loved to cheer his grandchildren on at sports and would encourage them by paying them a pound whenever they scored a goal or achieved a new personal best. Tom was always happy to help his grandchildren with whatever they needed. As they got older, they were happy to help their grandad too, offering tech support whenever he had a problem with his phone.

Just as his mother and Granny Fanny had taught him when he was a boy, Tom enjoyed teaching Georgia and Benjie how to cook, whipping up oat biscuits, Victoria sponges and Christmas cakes together.

Tom was happy to have family close by when he had to say goodbye to his dog Harry. Harry had been a loyal dog to Tom and a good friend to him while Pamela was ill.

On Top of the World

While Tom was very settled at home, his heart still yearned for adventure. In 2010 he booked a trip to Nepal to visit the Himalayan Mountains. There was one mountain he wished to see more than any other. The tallest mountain in the world, Mount Everest. Tom had caught his first glimpse of the Himalayas while visiting Gulmarg in northern India while on leave in 1944. Then, he could only see them in the distance and felt like he had to imagine the snow-capped peak of Everest. In 2010, Tom packed his suitcase to go on an adventure. His daughter Hannah dropped him off at the airport to fly to Kathmandu in Nepal. Seeing the mountains was a dream come true for Tom, and he booked a flight to take an even closer look. The pilot flew as high as he was allowed and didn't quite reach the top, but it was enough for Tom. At ninety years old, he was on top of the world and took lots of photographs to remember the trip.

In 2012, Tom took his daughters Lucy and Hannah to India to show them the country that had captured his heart all those years ago. They visited the home of Mahatma Gandhi and the Indian War Memorial Museum in the Red Fort.

Tom may have been getting older, but he was showing no signs of slowing down. Over the next few years, he jetted off to Italy with his regiment and to Cape Town, South Africa with his daughters. As well as his own travels he often joined Hannah and Lucy on their family holidays, too.

A Bad Fall

Even in his old age, Tom's life was full. He was busy and independent. However, all that came to an end in 2018 when he had an accident. Tom fell while he was unloading the dishwasher. The fall was a bad one. Tom was rushed to hospital, where the doctors confirmed he had broken a hip, several ribs and punctured his lung. Neither Tom's doctors nor his daughters were sure he would survive. Tom was ninety-eight years old and injuries as severe as his could be fatal for patients much younger than he was. Thanks to the wonderful care he received, Tom did survive. He did, however, have to spend two months recovering in hospital.

When the doctors thought Tom was well enough, he was moved to a rehabilitation centre. Here, the staff made him do exercises every day until he was ready to go home. Before that could happen, Tom's home needed to be made ready for him. To make sure Tom would be safe and happy at home, the NHS sent occupational therapists – healthcare professionals whose job it is to help people overcome the effects of disability or injury – to check his house to see how he would manage. Tom's bedroom was upstairs, and Tom's injuries made stairs very difficult for him. A stairlift was installed, which could carry him up or down the stairs whenever he needed. When everything was ready, Tom finally moved back home. Tom knew he had been very well looked after by all of the staff in the hospital and rehabilitation centre, but he was delighted to be home and with his family again. He was excited to get back to the life he had enjoyed before, though he knew, with his injuries, it wasn't going to be easy.

Tom was very grateful to be alive, but when he came out of hospital, his life was very different to the one he had before. Moving was difficult for him and he could no longer drive or be as independent as he had been. This was hard for Tom, who was so used to being able to help out around the house and mow the lawn on his ride-on mower. Tom was determined to do everything he could to get better and one thing he knew would help was exercise. Tom bought himself a treadmill that he could use in his room to speed up his rehabilitation. He hoped that the more he moved his legs the easier and less painful it would be. He also walked up and down the hallways of his house with his walking frame, trying to build up his strength.

A YEAR LIKE NO OTHER

While Tom's accident had stopped him from driving and mowing the lawn, some things in his life had not changed. Tom still got up early every morning, ate a breakfast of porridge made with condensed milk and read the newspaper. Tom may not have been able to get out and about as he used to but reading the paper and watching the news was his way of keeping in touch with what was going in the world.

Tom, like many other people, was watching the news in December 2019 when the first reports came in of a new and deadly virus outbreak in Wuhan, in the Hubei province of China. The virus was called COVID-19 and spread rapidly. Hospitals in Wuhan and the surrounding Hubei Province struggled to keep up with the growing number of severely ill patients. To help contain the virus, the city of Wuhan locked down, which meant people weren't allowed to leave the region and were only allowed to leave their homes for essential reasons. While these restrictions helped ease the pressure on hospitals in Wuhan, the virus was already out and starting to spread to other places.

Day after day, as more cases of COVID-19 were reported in other countries around the world, news of the disease took up more and more of Tom's newspaper, until it dominated the news in almost every country. As more people fell ill, hospitals in countries such as Italy, France and Spain filled up and soon became overwhelmed. Calls for ambulances went unanswered.

To help ease the pressure on hospitals and prevent further infection, governments took drastic measures. Lockdowns were imposed, which meant schools and all non-essential businesses were closed. People were only allowed to leave their homes to exercise or for essential purposes, such as buying food. People who could work at home were told to do so. Social distancing guidelines were issued, telling people not to meet up with others outside their household, including family members that lived in other homes. All gatherings, such as weddings, funerals and religious ceremonies, were strictly limited or even banned.

COVID-19 – FACTS

What is it: viruses are tiny particles that can cause disease. They are able to infect all living things. When outside of a host cell, a virus is harmless, but once inside a cell it is able to make copies of itself to infect other cells. Viruses can also change when they reproduce to create new versions of the virus called strains. These changes can make viruses able to infect other species. Many scientists believe that the current strain of the coronavirus originated in bats.

COVID-19 is one of a family of viruses called coronaviruses. Other coronaviruses include the common cold and various strains of influenza (flu). Coronaviruses get their name from the Latin word for crown or halo – *corona*. Scientists observing coronaviruses with powerful microscopes thought the virus particles looked like they had a crown of spikes on their surface.

Symptoms: tiredness, fever, cough and shortness of breath. Other symptoms can include the loss of taste and smell. While COVID-19 usually causes mild symptoms in young people, it can cause severe illness and even death to older people and people with underlying health conditions.

How it is transmitted: COVID-19 is transmitted by tiny droplets released into the air when an infected person coughs, sneezes or breathes heavily. A person becomes infected when these droplets come into contact with their nose or mouth either through breathing them in or by touching surfaces droplets have landed on and then touching their mouth, nose or eyes.

What makes COVID-19 a pandemic? A pandemic is when a disease can be found all over the world. Previous pandemics include the 1918 flu pandemic and the Black Death between 1665 and 1666.

UK scientists confirmed the first cases of COVID-19 in the United Kingdom on the 31 January 2020. By the end of February, more than twenty people had tested positive for the virus in the UK. The UK government hoped that the strict lockdown measures beginning to be imposed in other parts of the world could be avoided. They advised people to stay calm and to wash their hands thoroughly to prevent the spread of the disease. Unfortunately, these measures weren't enough.

As more cases of the disease were reported, hospitals began to fill. Soon, the number of deaths from the disease began to rise. It was clear that the situation was serious. The United Kingdom was on the brink of a health crisis unlike anything it had seen in over one hundred years.

Lockdown

On 23 March 2020, Prime Minister Boris Johnson made an announcement, calling on people in the UK to stay home to prevent the spread of the virus and save lives.

People were allowed to leave their homes to:

- shop for basic necessities

- perform one form of exercise per day, alone or with members of their household

- seek or provide care (medical or otherwise) for a vulnerable person

- travel to or from work if work could not be done from home.

People were not allowed to meet with friends or family members that they didn't live with. All non-essential shops closed. Social events were not allowed. All children, except those of critical workers were to be kept home from school.

CRITICAL WORKERS

Critical workers are people who have jobs that cannot be done at home and are essential for keeping others safe and healthy. Critical workers include health and social care workers, farmers, supermarket staff, police officers, teachers and transport workers.

The prime minister said that the government was doing everything it could to keep people safe from the virus by working to find a vaccine, rolling out a virus-testing program, setting up temporary hospitals and by giving resources to the NHS in order to treat the surging number of patients. However, he said that if people wanted to protect the NHS and frontline workers, they must obey the rules.

Protect the NHS

Not everyone agreed with the government's actions. Some people believed the government should have acted sooner and that the delay had cost thousands of lives. Other people didn't think the restrictions would make any positive difference. They thought that by not letting people go to work, or go shopping, the restrictions would damage the economy. One thing most people did agree on was the need to support the NHS. Hospitals around the country were struggling to meet the demand posed by COVID-19 with frontline workers such as doctors, nurses and paramedics being the hardest hit. Many more patients were being admitted, and there was a risk wards would run out of beds for them. Some patients needed a piece of specialist equipment, called a ventilator, to help with their breathing, and there were shortages of these too. NHS staff were working around the clock to give patients the best care they could, but they were pushed to the limit.

To show their thanks, at eight o'clock on 26 March 2020 people around the country stepped on to their doorsteps to give healthcare workers a well-deserved round of applause, to show appreciation for their hard work and to let them know that they were not forgotten.

Tom's Next Steps

Tom followed the developing story in the papers and on the news, which he watched with his family. As the country locked down, life for Tom remained much the same, but there were a few changes. As schools were closed, like children across the country, Tom's grandchildren Georgia and Benjie settled into distance learning. Hannah and Colin were home more than they were before the pandemic, too. Also, instead of going to the surgery, Tom's medical appointments took place online.

Another change for Tom was that his big one-hundredth birthday celebration, due to take place on 30 April 2020, had to be cancelled. Hannah and Lucy had planned a big family get together to celebrate their father, but with the new government restrictions, this would have to wait. Tom was disappointed, but as with any of the disappointments Tom had faced, he tried not to dwell on it. Tom was determined that when his birthday party did take place, he would be as fit as he could be.

Tom's family settled into lockdown as best they could. They were lucky to have a large house with lots of space for everybody, surrounded by a large garden. Over the winter, Tom hadn't spent much time in the garden because he still couldn't walk very well, and it was too cold to sit out there for very long. But on 5 April Tom decided to take his exercise outside and stepped into the warm sunshine. Little did Tom know that these were the first steps on an incredible journey that would change his life, and the life of his family, for ever.

"THE FIRST STEP WAS THE HARDEST. AFTER THAT, I GOT INTO THE SWING OF IT AND KEPT ON GOING."

Captain Sir Tom Moore

From the other side of the garden, Tom's son-in-law Colin was watching his efforts. Colin called out that Tom should try and do one hundred laps before his upcoming one hundredth birthday. Colin said that if Tom managed it, he would pay him a pound a lap to give to charity. Tom thought it was a wonderful idea, even though he wasn't sure whether he would be able to do one hundred laps. One thing he was sure of was that he wanted any money he raised to go towards NHS charities, to support the struggling health workers.

Tom was grateful for the care he had received in hospital and the care the NHS had provided his family over the years. Tom saw on the news and read in the papers how the COVID-19 pandemic had put the healthcare system under massive stress. Doctors and nurses were working day and night and doing everything they could to battle against the virus. Tom compared their efforts to his own experiences during World War Two.

"At that time, the people my age, we were fighting on the front line and the general public was standing behind us," Tom said. "In this instance, the doctors and nurses and all the medical people, they're the front line. It's up to my generation to back them up, just as we were backed up."

During World War Two everyone was encouraged to "do their bit" to help the war effort. At home, that could mean volunteering to watch for fires or digging up your lawn or flower garden to grow vegetables. In the battle against COVID-19, Tom couldn't ride a motorcycle or drive a tank. He couldn't even ride his trusty lawn mower. But Tom could walk, and so he did. But he didn't do it all at once. Tom's garden was twenty-five metres (eighty-two feet) long. Tom knew he couldn't do 2,500 metres in one go, instead Tom broke the walk down into groups of ten laps.

Local News

Hannah suggested they turn Tom's walk into a campaign and put it up on the online fundraising platform JustGiving.com to raise £1,000. To let people know about Tom's plan, Hannah wrote a short press release and sent it to the local newspaper in their area. Tom's grandson Benjie asked people to support him on social media, setting up and managing a Twitter account for Tom. Soon afterwards, they were contacted by a local news programme, who did a small feature on Tom's one-hundreth Birthday Walk for the NHS. When people heard about what Tom was doing, they donated money to help him reach his goal and used social media to encourage their friends and followers to do the same. To begin with, the donations were small, but as more and more people donated and shared Tom's story the total on the JustGiving.com page rose quickly.

GOING VIRAL

By 10 April, donations to Tom's JustGiving page already exceeded the £1,000 target. The family raised it to £5,000 and then shortly after to a staggering £500,000. Donations soon blew through this target too. People touched by Tom's story shared it with friends and family on social media. News stations around the country started to pay attention.

On 12 April, Tom was invited to appear on British singer and presenter Michael Ball's programme on Radio 2. Something about Tom's walk caught people's imagination. With so many dramatic news stories about the virus, Tom's quiet walk around his garden to raise money for healthcare workers was a perfect antidote. Hannah had hoped the story might be a small thing that brought people "a little bit of joy" but did not imagine the scale of the impact it would have. Within days, the world's media descended on their house and filled up their driveway, all keen to follow the story. Soon Hannah and Tom had more than a million emails. People wanted to know more about Captain Tom and his family.

Soon Tom and Hannah were doing as many as thirty interviews a day for news networks all over the world. Hannah sat beside Tom for interviews to make sure he heard the questions and to repeat them if he needed her to, just as Tom had done for his father when he was young. Hannah also conducted many interviews herself. It was hard work, but with every interview, the amount of money raised for the NHS leaped up. Celebrities tweeted their support and encouraged their followers and fans to donate to Tom's appeal.

"EVERYONE IS INSPIRED BY HIS STORY AND HIS DETERMINATION. HE'S A ONE-MAN FUNDRAISING

MACHINE. GOD KNOWS WHAT THE FINAL TOTAL WILL BE."

Prince William

Soon they had reached more than a £1 million. Tom and Hannah couldn't believe what was happening, but support for Tom and the amount of money being donated kept on growing.

As well as this, Tom kept on walking. It was hard, but knowing all the money he was raising was for a cause so close to his heart, helped keep him motivated.

As Tom completed his one hundredth lap on the morning of 16 April, he was joined by a television crew to capture the moment. Tom's

Captain Tom completes his walk

garden was lined by a guard of honour, sent by the 1st Battalion of the Yorkshire Regiment, who wanted to honour a veteran who had answered the call of duty yet again. By this time, the total stood at a staggering £5 million, and it was still going up. At one point the total was increasing by about £5,000 per minute, with donations pouring in from all over the world for amounts as little as a pound to several thousand. No matter what the amount, the donors all wished Tom well. He had completed his walk, but Tom's fundraising wasn't over yet. The total was still rising, and Tom had other money-making ideas.

Making Records

To celebrate Tom's one hundredth lap, singer Michael Ball sang to Tom on *BBC Breakfast*, "You'll Never Walk Alone", originally from the musical *Carousel*. Tom loved it and agreed to record a version of the song with Michael Ball and the NHS Voices of Care Choir. The plan was to release it as a single to raise money. The track, with Tom speaking the lyrics, was released the very next day and quickly became one of the fastest-selling and most-streamed songs the country had ever seen.

On 23 April, Tom made a very special appearance on ITV's *Good Morning Britain*. Under the impression he was there to speak to the presenters about his walk and fundraising efforts, Tom was surprised when he was presented with a Pride of Britain Award, which honours those who have acted bravely in challenging circumstances.

PRIDE OF BRITAIN AWARDS

The Pride of Britain Awards is a ceremony that takes place each year in the United Kingdom to celebrate the achievements of ordinary people who have acted bravely or contributed to society in an extraordinary way. The winners of the awards are selected from many thousands of nominations sent in by the public.

Tom was delighted because he was a big fan of the awards and the people who won them.

"I've always had great pride in Britain. I'm very proud to be British and to be given a Pride of Britain Award is really outstanding … never in a hundred years did I ever anticipate that the award would be given to me."

On 24 April, Tom became a record breaker yet again when he became the oldest person to reach number one in the Official Singles Chart, taking the crown from the previous record holder, Sir Tom Jones. It also meant that Tom was top of the charts on his one hundredth birthday.

A Very Special Birthday

When the prime minister had announced a national lockdown at the end of March 2020, Tom's family were disappointed because it meant having to cancel their plans for Tom's one hundredth birthday party. Little did they know that, instead of a family party, the whole country and many other people around the world would be celebrating alongside them. As well as cake and cards with Hannah and her family in Bedfordshire, and an onscreen visit with Lucy and her family in Caversham, Tom was treated to a day filled with celebrations.

FLY PAST On the morning of his birthday, Tom was treated to a fly past by two World War Two aeroplanes, a Hurricane and Spitfire, flown by RAF pilots.

CARDS As well as birthday cards from Her Majesty Queen Elizabeth and Prime Minister Boris Johnson, Tom was sent more than 125,000 cards from people all over the world. This was far too many for Tom to have at home. Instead, the head teacher at Benjie's school allowed them to be displayed in the school hall.

VISITS The commanding officer of the 1st Battalion of the Yorkshire Regiment had a special letter for Tom informing him that he had been promoted from captain to honorary colonel of the Harrogate Army Foundation College in Yorkshire. He told Tom that he hoped Tom's achievement would inspire future junior leaders in the army. Tom was honoured. He said he would always be known as Captain Tom, but if people wanted to call him colonel he would say, "thank you very much".

MEDALS The army had another surprise for him. In many of Captain Tom's television appearances, he wore three medals attached to his jacket. Tom had been awarded four medals after the war, and a member of the Ministry of Defence Medal Office had noticed that one was missing. Tom was awarded the Defence Medal 1939–1945 he had lost, to wear proudly alongside his others. Captain Tom was overwhelmed and grateful for the honour that was awarded him by an organization he had worked so hard to serve.

BIRTHDAY MESSAGES Messages from people all over the world poured in, wishing Tom a happy birthday, including one from Prime Minister Boris Johnson who said, "Your heroic efforts have lifted the spirits of the entire nation."

CAKES No birthday would be complete without a birthday cake. Tom's favourite cake was a simple Victoria sponge filled with jam, but he got more than that. He received all sorts of cakes, including a few with his portrait on and some with a miniature Captain Tom modelled in fondant. Famous chef Jamie Oliver even baked a coffee and walnut cake to celebrate. As much as Tom would have liked to, there was no way he could eat all the delicious treats he was given, so he donated them to hospitals and care homes nearby.

Tom's family closed donations to the JustGiving page at the end of the day, with the total at a staggering £32.8 million. It was a record-breaking sum, more than any single fundraiser had ever raised.

NHS CHARITIES TOGETHER

NHS Charities Together is a national charity caring for the NHS. It is made up of 241 member charities that help provide extra support to hospital trusts, ambulance trusts and community health trusts.

The money raised by Tom's walk was used to address the needs of patients and staff. It provided staff with hot meals when they needed them, and practical things such as appliances for staff areas, like fridges and microwaves. Funds have been used to support workers across the NHS – providing counselling services for staff impacted by COVID-19 to allow them to talk about how working on the front line of healthcare and having to make life and death decisions affected their mental health.

As well as raising money himself, Tom's walk inspired others to raise money too. It is estimated that COVID-19 fundraising has raised more than £100 million. Tom's efforts also reminded patients and staff that they were not forgotten; that even though they couldn't get together with people they loved, people were thinking about them and appreciated everything they were doing.

"CAPTAIN SIR TOM INSPIRED SO MANY PEOPLE TO TAKE ON THEIR OWN EXTRAORDINARY CHALLENGES, FROM RUNNING MARATHONS TO SWIMMING LAKES, AND HE GAVE US ALL HOPE. HE SHOWED NHS PATIENTS AND STAFF WHO WERE STRUGGLING THAT PEOPLE CARED, THAT THEY

WERE LOOKING OUT FOR THEM AND DOING WHAT THEY COULD TO SUPPORT THEM."

Ellie Orton, Chief Executive
of NHS Charities Together

THE AFTER PARTY

After a whirlwind few months of fundraising and interviews, no one would have blamed Captain Tom if he had taken a break, but Tom didn't want to. Before his birthday, as the total on his JustGiving stretched into the millions, Tom and his family had sat together to decide what they wanted to do next. As Prince William had said, Tom was a "fundraising machine", and he had no intention of stopping. Tom and his family decided to set up a foundation called the Captain Tom Foundation, which would not only continue to raise money for NHS charities, but would also provide support for people who were bereaved or lonely, and champion education equality.

As well as setting up his own foundation, Tom was still busy doing interviews. Interest in Tom and what he had achieved continued to grow, even after he had finished his walk. Now instead of his campaign, people wanted to find out more about his inspiring personality.

Team Player

In July 2020, Tom got a visit from former England football team captain, David Beckham. To honour Tom for what he had achieved on behalf on NHS Charities Together, David awarded Tom his very own England jersey for the Lionhearts, a team of inspirational heroes. The Lionhearts squad was set up to celebrate those who went above and beyond to make a positive contribution during the challenging time of the COVID-19 pandemic. When they sat together, David asked Tom what he thought made a good leader. Tom answered, "...you have to realize there is good in everyone." Fellow Lionhearts included fitness instructor Joe Wicks and fundraiser Tony Hudgell (see page 190).

Oh, What a Knight

On 17 July, Tom was invited to Windsor Castle to receive an honour which eclipsed the many others he had been awarded. He was to be knighted by Queen Elizabeth II herself in her first official engagement after lockdown.

Knighted by the Queen

The ceremony was unique because it took place at Windsor Castle, where Her Majesty had spent lockdown, on the lawn, rather than inside Buckingham Palace. Also, during the ceremony it is customary for the person being knighted to kneel before the queen, but Tom was allowed to stand because his injuries made kneeling very difficult. Tom worried that if he knelt down, he might not be able to stand up again and have to be "hauled up by a crane".

Tom was honoured and said that it was a dream to stand so close to the Queen, a woman he had admired for many years. It was something he would "never ever forget ... for the rest of my life."

In August 2020, as part of their commemoration of the seventy-fifth anniversary of Victory in Europe Day (VE Day) the National Army Museum unveiled a portrait of Captain Tom painted by artist Alex Chamberlin.

Captain Tom's Story

Somehow, amidst all the interviews and awards, Tom found the time to write down all he remembered about his life, from his childhood in Yorkshire to his time serving in India and Burma. He wrote about his many jobs, his marriages – both happy and sad – all the way up to becoming a knight of the realm. Tom named his autobiography *Tomorrow Will Be a Good Day* because that was a phrase he always said to himself to get through difficult times. Tom's book was published on 17 September 2020 and became an immediate bestseller. Readers loved Tom's story and the optimism with which he faced the many challenges he encountered in his life.

Tom's story was so inspiring that film companies competed over who would be allowed to turn it into a film. On 23 September, Captain Sir Tom signed a deal with a film company to give them permission to do just that. Tom was amazed but joked that he didn't know any one-hundred-year-old actors still fit enough to play him.

Man of the Year

If that wasn't enough, Tom also became a magazine cover star when he was voted one of *GQ*'s Men of the Year at their twenty-third Men of the Year awards. Tom appeared wearing a black suit and bow tie with a Union Jack draped around his shoulders. As well as an interview inside the magazine, Tom also appeared in a very funny clip for the ceremony about how he kept in shape. In the clip, Tom steps away from his famous walking frame before running, jumping, skateboarding and even working on his back flip. While Tom didn't perform any of the stunts himself, he did provide the voiceover with his classic dry sense of humour.

In December 2020, Captain Tom took centre stage, or rather centre screen, at the 2020 Royal Variety Performance, along with the NHS Voices of Care Choir and Michael Ball. Together, they performed their lockdown anthem, "You'll Never Walk Alone". The powerful words spoke to the nation, as they sang, "walk on through the wind, walk on through the rain." Like the song, Captain Tom had walked on through all his troubles, onward to a better day and, just as the song said, he did not walk alone. He had the whole nation willing him on, not just to support him, or to support the NHS, but to support everyone who had lost so much that year and who faced so much uncertainty.

An Unexpected Adventure

With the COVID-19 pandemic, 2020 had been a year of change for everyone, none more so than

Captain Tom and his family. As 2020 came to an end, Tom's life couldn't have been more different from when the year had started. From being a beloved grandfather, struggling to walk to the end of his garden and get back his independence, he was now a national celebrity. He'd gone from a respected captain, having served his country in some of the most difficult and dangerous battles of World War Two, to an honorary colonel and knight of the realm. It had been a busy year and, while it had been good fun, it had also been hard work. Tom and his family needed a holiday.

Tom didn't think he would get the chance to travel again, not only because of his health, but also because of COVID-19 travel restrictions imposed by the government to help prevent the spread of the virus. For much of the year, travel abroad had been off limits to most people, unless they had an essential reason to visit another country. But in December, travel corridors opened up between areas that the government believed it was safe to travel to. One of these countries was Barbados in the Caribbean. In recognition of Tom and his family's fundraising achievements and hard work, British Airways gifted Tom a flight to Barbados so they could spend time together in the sunshine. The trip would also give Tom a chance to relax away from all the attention and interviews.

Tom's Last Battle

Captain Tom had a wonderful holiday but began to feel unwell not long after he returned home. Tom had developed a lung infection called pneumonia, which made it difficult for Tom to breathe. Doctors prescribed medicine to help him get better. Tom's family hoped he would recover at home, but as his condition worsened they decided he needed to go to hospital. Tom was admitted to Bedford Hospital on 31 January 2021. At the hospital the doctors discovered that Tom's pneumonia was worse than they thought. He also tested positive for COVID-19. Although vaccines for COVID-19 were available at this time, Tom was too ill to receive one. When Tom's daughter Hannah released the news, people all over the world sent get well messages and tributes to Tom and his family.

Staff at the hospital did everything they could, but the infection was too much for Tom. On 2 February 2021, after saying goodbye to his daughter Lucy and the family on FaceTime, and with his daughter Hannah at his side, Tom died.

After his death, Hannah and Lucy released a statement:

"WHILST HE'D BEEN IN SO MANY HEARTS FOR JUST A SHORT TIME, HE WAS AN INCREDIBLE FATHER AND GRANDFATHER, AND HE WILL STAY ALIVE IN OUR HEARTS FOREVER."

A World of Gratitude

· ·

Many people had followed Captain Sir Tom's story and after he died tributes poured in from up and down the country and all over the world. The Union Jack was lowered to half-mast at Number 10 Downing Street in London. Prime Minister Boris Johnson released a statement:

"CAPTAIN SIR TOM MOORE WAS A HERO IN THE TRUEST SENSE OF THE WORD. IN THE DARK DAYS OF THE SECOND WORLD WAR, HE FOUGHT FOR FREEDOM AND IN THE FACE OF THIS COUNTRY'S DEEPEST POST-WAR CRISIS HE UNITED US ALL, HE CHEERED US ALL UP, AND HE EMBODIED THE TRIUMPH

OF THE HUMAN SPIRIT. HE BECAME NOT JUST A NATIONAL INSPIRATION BUT A BEACON OF HOPE FOR THE WORLD."

In the USA, the White House tweeted,

"WE JOIN THE UNITED KINGDOM AND THE WORLD IN HONOURING THE MEMORY OF CAPTAIN SIR TOM MOORE, WHO INSPIRED MILLIONS THROUGH HIS LIFE AND HIS ACTIONS."

On hearing of Captain Sir Tom's death, the British Army tweeted that he was "an exceptional man and soldier to the end."

A Final Farewell

....

At 6 o'clock on 3 February 2021, the day after Tom died, the people of Great Britain took to their doorsteps again, this time to clap for Captain Sir Tom Moore. They clapped to say thank you to a man who had served his country more than once, and whose small act of walking in his garden not only raised a great deal of money, but also raised spirits. He had sent people a message of hope and positivity when they needed it most.

Before he died, Tom had joked with Lucy and Hannah that after this year, his funeral might have to be a bit bigger than they had planned. Tom told them that he wanted there to be a Victoria sponge and sandwiches after the service, and that he was very relieved he wouldn't have to make them.

Due to COVID-19 restrictions and the family's wishes, Tom's funeral was a small family service. But even though people could not join the family in person, many watched on television. Tom's family shared memories of Tom who, though a hero to so many, was their beloved father and grandad. Tom's ashes were taken up to the family grave in Yorkshire so he could be with his mother and father again, near the countryside where he grew up.

"SO EVEN IF TOMORROW IS MY LAST DAY, IF ALL THOSE I LOVED ARE WAITING FOR ME THEN THAT TOMORROW WILL BE A GOOD DAY TOO."

Captain Sir Tom Moore

TOM WALKS ON

Captain Sir Tom Moore was one hundred years old when he died, an age many consider to be very old indeed, but Tom proved it is never too late to do something to make the world a better place. Inspired by Tom, people from all over the world, of all ages and abilities, thought up ways they could raise money for charity.

As well as raising an enormous sum for charity and setting up the Captain Tom Foundation, part of Captain Sir Tom's legacy is how his garden walk inspired other people to think about what they could contribute.

104-year-old Ruth Saunders from Newbury, Berkshire raised more than £31,000 for the Thames Valley Ambulance Service by walking laps of her home, totalling a distance of forty-two kilometres (twenty-six miles). When she completed the distance, Ruth said she was relieved. "When I start at something I always want to finish it, no matter what it is."

Rhythwyn Evans from Ceridigion, Wales, raised more than £3,000 for his local NHS charity. With the help of his walking stick, the ninety-one-year-old walked ninety-one laps around his bungalow. "I want to give something back to the area that I've always lived."

At the beginning of 2020, five-year-old Tony Hudgell received a new pair of prosthetic legs from the NHS. Near-fatal injuries meant Tony had his legs amputated when he was just a baby. Tony's mum hoped that his new legs would help him to be able to walk. Tony wasn't sure he wanted to try them, but when he saw Captain Tom walking with his frame on television, Tony told his mum that he could do what Tom was doing – and so he did. Tony set out to raise £500 for the Evelina Children's Hospital by walking ten kilometres (six miles). Tony raised much more than that and he walked further too, instead of stopping at ten kilometres Tony walked thirteen (eight miles). Tony's walk raised £1.5 million. Tony's mum said that if it hadn't been for Captain Tom, she didn't think that Tony would be walking at all now, but after watching Tom persevere for a good cause Tony is now able to play with his friends in the playground.

Dabirul Islam Choudhury, from Bow, London, hoped to raise £1,000 by walking one hundred laps of his communal garden, while fasting during the month of Ramadan. The 101-year-old raised more then £420,000 for the families of victims of COVID-19. In recognition of his achievements, Dabirul was awarded an OBE from Her Majesty the Queen and congratulated by Captain Sir Tom himself.

Margaret Payne from Ardvar in the Scottish Highlands raised more than £375,000 for the NHS, Highland Hospice and Royal National Lifeboat Institution (RNLI). Ninety-year-old Margaret raised the money by climbing her stairs 282 times, the equivalent of climbing 731 metres (2,400 feet), which is the height of Suilven, a Scottish mountain she had climbed when she was just fifteen.

Tom had been a fundraiser all of his life, for the Round Table, for and later for NHS Charities Together. Tom wanted his spirit of community service to keep on going after his death and with the Captain Tom Foundation he could do just that.

Captain Tom's 100 Challenge

While Captain Tom's funeral was a quiet family affair, the Captain Tom Foundation planned a celebration of his life on 30 April 2021, on what would have been Captain Tom's 101st birthday.

"WE WILL MAKE SURE IT IS AN EVENT THAT EVERYONE – IN THE UK AND AROUND THE WORLD – CAN GET INVOLVED IN AND IT WILL TRULY CELEBRATE HIS GENEROSITY OF SPIRIT, THE HOPE AND JOY HE BROUGHT TO MILLIONS AND HIS SENSE OF FUN."

Hannah Ingram-Moore

To celebrate Tom on what would have been his 101st birthday, his family and the Captain

Tom Foundation set up the "Captain Tom 100 Challenge" in which they challenged people to do one hundred things to raise money for charity, just as Captain Sir Tom had walked one hundred laps of his garden.

Hannah said that she and the family had spoken with her father about the work of the foundation and their idea for the "100 Challenge" and that he was firmly behind it and had hoped he would be able to take part in it himself. Sadly, that wasn't to be.

Walking in Tom's Footsteps

To get the ball rolling, on the morning of 30 April 2021, Captain Tom's daughter, Hannah Ingram-Moore stepped out into her garden with her son Benjie and her daughter, Georgia to walk one hundred laps of their garden, just as her father had done a little over a year before.

And they weren't alone. Inspired by Captain Tom and the work of the foundation, people up and down the country and all over the world took up the Captain Tom 100 Challenge.

- Actor Dame Judi Dench ate one hundred of her favourite chocolates.
- Former England football captain, David Beckham did one hundred keepy-uppies.
- Athlete Dame Jessica Ennis-Hill attempted one hundred pogo jumps.
- Former *Great British Bake-Off* judge Dame Mary Berry said she would make one hundred cakes.

As well as celebrities, children in schools across the country walked one hundred laps of their play grounds, attempted to shoot one hundred basketballs and score one hundred goals, all inspired by the Captain Tom 100 Challenge.

- Children at a primary school in Cornwall planted one hundred seeds on the school grounds.
- Children at a junior school in Peterborough did one hundred star jumps on the playground.

- Children at a school in Norfolk cut out one hundred hand shapes in rainbow colours to make an artwork of inspirational quotes.

Hannah said the event was "tinged with a little sadness" but that she wanted it to be about "hope for the future and ensuring his lasting legacy of hope".

An Inspiring Legacy

The Captain Tom 100 was a huge success not only for raising money for charity but also for proving what Captain Tom always believed to be true, that no matter how old or young a person is or what struggles they may have, there is always something they can do to make the world a better place for others and have some fun along the way.

Captain Tom may not have been able to take part in the 100 Challenge, but his legacy of hope and doing whatever you can to serve the community lives on in the work of the Captain Tom Foundation and the fundraising efforts of the many people he inspired.

TIMELINE OF CAPTAIN TOM MOORE'S LIFE

1920 Thomas Moore is born on 30 April in Keighley, Yorkshire to Isabella and Wilfred Moore

1933 Adolf Hitler becomes chancellor of Germany

1935 Tom finishes school, aged fifteen, and begins an apprenticeship with a water engineering company

1936 The German *Hindenburg* airship flies over Keighley

1939 Germany invades Poland. British prime minister, Neville Chamberlain, announces that Britain is at war with Germany two days later. World War Two begins

1940 Tom signs up to join the army. He is conscripted into the 8th Battalion, Duke of Wellington's Regiment

1941 Tom is promoted to second lieutenant and becomes an officer

1941 Tom travels to Myanmar (then Burma) in October where he learns to drive a tank with the 50th Indian Tank Brigade

1944 Tom is promoted to captain

1945 Tom returns to England, where he learns to operate and repair Churchill tanks

1945 On 8 May, Germany surrenders and victory is declared in Europe

1945 Japan surrenders on 15 August and World War Two ends

1946 Tom leaves the army and begins working for the family building firm, W. Moore and Son

1949 Tom meets Billie, and the pair soon get married

1959 After W. Moore and Son closes down, Tom starts working at a local quarry

1960 Tom becomes a travelling salesman for building supplies company, Nuralite

1967 Tom and Billie separate

1968 Tom marries his second wife, Pamela

1968 Tom and Pamela's first child, Lucy, is born

1970 Tom and Pamela's second child, Hannah, is born

1989 Tom and Pamela buy a villa in Burgos, Spain and move there with Hannah

1993 Tom and Pamela move back to England. Pamela is diagnosed with dementia

2006 Tom's wife, Pamela, dies

2007 Tom organizes the 60th reunion of the Duke of Wellington's Regiment. He moves in with his daughter Hannah, her husband, Colin, and their two children Georgia and Benjie

2010 Tom visits Nepal and takes a flight over Mount Everest

2018 Tom has an accident and breaks his hip, along with several ribs. He spends two months in hospital, then returns home to continue his rehabilitation

2019 In December reports of a new coronavirus disease, COVID-19, circulate. The first cases come from Wuhan, China but the disease quickly spreads around the world

2020 On 23 March, Prime Minister Boris Johnson asks people in the UK to stay at home in order to protect the NHS and save lives during the COVID-19 pandemic

2020 On 4 April, Tom decides to walk one hundred laps of his garden in order to raise money for doctors and nurses of the NHS

2020 Tom completes his one hundredth lap of the garden on 16 April. In total, Tom raises £32.8 million

2020 On 24 April, Tom becomes the oldest person to reach number one in the Official Singles Chart with "You'll Never Walk Alone"

2020 Tom celebrates his one hundredth birthday on 30 April. He received over 125,000 birthday cards, including one from Prime Minister Boris Johnson and one from the Queen

2020 Tom is knighted on 17 July. He becomes Captain Sir Thomas Moore

2020 On 17 September, Tom's autobiography, *Tomorrow Will Be a Good Day*, is published

2021 On 2 February, after catching pneumonia, then testing positive for COVID-19, Captain Sir Tom Moore dies

2021 The Captain Tom Foundation holds a celebration of his life on what would have been Tom's 101st birthday on 30 April. People around the world take part in the "Captain Tom 100 Challenge" – a challenge to do one hundred things to raise money for charity

ABOUT THE AUTHOR

Sally Morgan was born in Malaysia but grew up in England. She studied Literature and Classics at university. After graduating, she worked as a bookseller and editor before becoming a full-time writer. She is the author of many books including *Dream Big* and the My Best Friend series. Sally lives in Minneapolis with her husband and two children.

A SHORT HISTORY OF THE NHS

The National Health Service, known as the NHS, is in charge of keeping people in the UK healthy. The service is run by the government and paid for by taxes, which means it's free to use at the time you need to use it. It is open to all residents in the UK – rich or poor, young or old.

During the early twentieth century, healthcare in the UK had a lot of problems. If someone was ill or needed a doctor, they usually had to pay for treatment. This meant that many poor people didn't get the help they needed, because they couldn't afford it. It was an old-fashioned system, started back in Victorian times when poor people were not looked after very well in society. Sometimes, people had health insurance through their jobs, which meant that they could access healthcare services for lower costs or for free. However, their families usually weren't covered by this insurance.

Healthcare services were run by local councils or private companies, and some hospitals and surgeries were much better than others, depending on where in the country they were. This meant you might have to pay more for worse treatment, depending on where you lived!

World War Two put plans for healthcare reform on hold, but after the fighting had finished, the government decided it was time for change. They believed that medical help should be given based on who needed it, rather than who could pay for it. The National Health Service was started in 1948 under Minister of Health Aneurin Bevan. It brought together many healthcare services, including surgeries, hospitals, pharmacies, dentists and opticians, under a national system. It provided people all over the UK with medical care. Over the following decades, the

NHS made many medical breakthroughs. Here are just a few of them:

• In 1958, the NHS rolled out its first major vaccination programme, offering injections for polio and diphtheria. Before these vaccinations, as many as 5,000 people could die of these diseases during an outbreak. Thanks to the vaccination programme, nobody has died of polio or diphtheria in the UK since the 1970s.
• In 1968, the first UK heart transplant was conducted by NHS doctors.
• In 1978, the world's first baby was born through in vitro fertilisation (IVF) at an NHS hospital.

Today, the NHS is the fifth largest employer in the world, with over 1.7 million people working for it. The biggest group is nurses, but there are many different roles including doctors, surgeons, hospital managers, paramedics, occupational therapists, cleaners and IT consultants. Though the NHS is now twelve times more expensive to run than it was in 1948, it is still mostly free to use, but in England there are charges for prescriptions, along with dental work.

During the COVID-19 pandemic, NHS workers were put under enormous pressure as many people became seriously ill with the disease. Every Thursday for ten weeks during lockdown, members of the public stepped out on to their doorsteps to clap for the NHS heroes and show their appreciation.

GLOSSARY

Airship: an aircraft that is kept afloat by a gas which is lighter than air, such as helium or hydrogen.

Antibiotics: medicines that kill harmful bacteria and stop it from spreading, preventing infections.

Bacteria: tiny living things that live on us, around us and in us. Most bacteria are harmless, but some can cause illness, infection or disease.

Biplane: a type of plane with two pairs of wings, one above the other.

Colony: an area or country under the control of another country, occupied by settlers from the controlling country.

Conscription: when a government instructs people to join the armed forces, usually during a war. This is to ensure the army, navy and air force are strong enough to fight.

Convoy: a group of vehicles travelling together for protection.

Coronavirus: coronaviruses are a group of viruses that cause illnesses in humans and animals. They often affect the respiratory system.

COVID-19: a disease in humans caused by a coronavirus. Symptoms can include a high temperature, persistent cough and difficulty breathing.

Dementia: a condition or illness that affects the way the brain works. It can cause changes in the way a person thinks and what they can remember.

Influenza (flu): an infection caused by a virus, which is easily passed from person to person. Symptoms include body aches and fever.

Monument: a building or statue, put up to celebrate or commemorate a special person or event.

Pandemic: an outbreak of a disease which spreads across the world.

Propaganda: information which spreads ideas intended to make people feel a certain way or support a particular cause.

Quarantine: isolation of people or animals to prevent the spread of disease.

Rationing: a system of limiting people's access to food, fuel and clothes due to shortages, usually carried out during wartime.

Rehabilitation: the process of getting back in good health after an illness, accident or addiction.

Surveillance: watching someone or something closely, such as spying on enemy activity during a war.

Symptoms: a physical sign of a disease or condition, such as a high temperature or runny nose.

Transmitted: passed on from one person or place to another.

Treaty: a formal agreement made between countries.

Vaccination: a way to prevent the spread of disease. An injection or tablet which triggers the body's immune response to fight off the disease.

Ventilators: a machine that helps people breathe, or breathes for them.

Veteran: a former member of the armed forces.

Virus: tiny particles that cause disease in people and animals, such as influenza or COVID-19.

BIBLIOGRAPHY AND
FURTHER READING

Thank You, Heroes
Hegarty, Patricia and Emmerson, Michael (2020)
Caterpillar Books

Coronavirus: A Book for Children about COVID-19
Jenner, Elizabeth, Roberts, Nia, Wilson, Kate
and Scheffler, Axel (2020)
Nosy Crow

Tomorrow Will Be a Good Day
Moore, Captain Tom (2020)
Michael Joseph

Home Again: Stories About Coming Home from War
Various authors (2020)
Scholastic

INDEX